Voices from the Other
Side *of the* Couch

Voices from the Other Side *of the* Couch

A Warrior's View of Shamanic Healing

John Myerson

and

Judith Robbins

Also co-authored
by
John Myerson

Riding the Spirit Wind

Stories of Shamanic Healing

Address inquiries to:
LifeArts Press
WayoftheRedDragon.com
Printed in the United States of America

First Edition 2008
ISBN 978-0-9816420-7-9
EPUB: 978-0-9816420-4-8

Voices from the Other Side of the Couch:
A Warrior's View of Shamanic Healing
John G. Myerson and Judith Robbins

PLEASE NOTE
The cases described in this book are composites. They have been
deliberately combined and altered in order to protect John Myerson's
patients' rights of confidentiality and privacy.
No one found in this book corresponds to any actual person, living or dead.

This Book is dedicated to John's wife,

LAURA TALMUD

with our love.

Acknowledgments

As is the nature of all things, we have been connected to and supported by many people.

We thank the Way of Power groups of the LifeArts Community and the patients who have shared their souls with John. This book is a direct result of their kindness.

We would like to thank our teachers, who shared their hearts and the Dharma connections passed down through the generations.

Many thanks to our patient, astute, and helpful readers: Aaron Askinase, Paul Gallagher, Jan Hastings, Anne Keaney, Maria Pizarro, and Judy Seidl.

We would like to express our thanks to Harry and Marjorie for their kindness in designing our book.

From John, special thanks to the men—Bruce Berlent, Andy Osborne, Peter Ostrow, Mark Halperin, and Paul Weisman—for their love and support. To Christine Lee for her love, compassion, and healing. I want to thank my dear friend John Shelton for always being there with support, ideas, positive energy, and love when I needed him the most. Particular thanks to Amelia Kinkade for your many lifetimes of watching my back, critical feedback, and blue light. It is hard to find people who are loyal, trustworthy, and with honor. I have been very fortunate.

From Judy, special thanks to you who have given me laughter through the smooth parts and encouragement through the rough, wisdom, and kindness through all—Jonathan Ceely; Anne Keaney; Tyler Knowles; Bonnie Levy; Larry, Wendy, and Liz Robbins. And love to Stanton, Denise, Ben, and Rachel for being who you are.

We want to express our gratitude for being able to work together on this project. We have both learned a great deal and are privileged to be able to make this offering.

Contents

Introduction

There's a big couch in my office, forest green with dark gold stripes. People who come to see me usually sit there to talk and tell their stories. But I don't hear only the person sitting across from me. I am always amazed at how many other voices are present when I am talking to people. Some talk to me as you would, others seem to come from visions, and still others just appear in my mind. They seem to come from the other side of the couch, hovering in my mind just out of normal means of perception. They come from another world, a real world, but different from the ordinary reality of two people just sitting and talking. Learning how people connect to this other world, this greater world of the Universe, is what this book is all about.

There are infinite ways to connect to what I call the Universe. The word *Universe* is just the term I use for what others may call God, Tao, Great Spirit, Goddess, and Creative Spirit. It doesn't matter what you call it. Not only are there different names for this creative energy, but there are also different ways to connect to it. Some people like to dance; others prefer to be still. Some like silence, some like loud drums. Some feel they journey out to other realms while some feel they go deep inside themselves. What works for you depends on your nature.

The way you connect to the Universe has a cultural component as well. Christians may see angels, Native Americans may see animal spirits, yet others may sense souls or spirit guides drawn from their own cultures. I have worked with people who see space people, aliens, and lizard creatures. None of it really matters; for me all manifestations are the same. The One is the same for all of us. It's just that our perception and the expression of this Universal energy will be colored by who and what we are.

This being the case, I am surprised at how people get attached to the one way they connect to the Universe. Over time, they may come to believe that because their way works for them, their way is the only way.

In truth, all ways are valid, so in my work with individuals or groups, I try to help people find their individual ways of connecting to the Universe. Some will look like mine; and some will be completely different. It's important as a teacher to make space for the different ways and not to fall into the temptation of making little clones of one's self, insisting that one's own way is the only way. And it's important for everyone not to be rigid about or to deny other people's ways of connecting to the Universe. Each way has its own benefit.

In this book, I'll be telling stories and giving descriptions of some patterns or archetypes I have come across in my years of practice. These are the voices that come from the other side of the couch. You may find that some of them may help you see your own patterns and that some may help you on your way. But the book is by no means all-inclusive; there are infinite ways to go about this. I have just brought some of the main patterns that I've seen.

The patterns describe ways that people connect to the Universe, find their own power, and express their own gifts. I've talked as if the patterns are distinct, as if a person has just one pattern. In fact, a person is likely to have more than one, to move from one to another, and to use one gift or another in different circumstances. Nonetheless, everyone has a dominant gift even if others are present as well. For example, I may be primarily a Warrior, but I'm likely to hyperfocus to see what's going on with someone, then take action as a Warrior, and then move to using the energy of love to help him heal.

I've articulated the patterns as if they're totally separate modes of being because it's difficult to describe the way the energy of the Universe flows through us and enables us to have our individual powers. We have to stop the flow in order to describe it. Take an analogy: an electron doesn't exist as a piece of matter, it's more like a probability of being in a certain place at a certain time; it's more like energy or a cloud than like a hunk of something. But to teach about electrons, we say an atom has one or two or three electrons moving around a nucleus in a distinct orbit like a planet around a sun. Similarly, the patterns in the book are descriptions of some ways in which the energy of the Universe can flow.

To shift the analogy, the way the energy of the Universe moves through us is like a stream that flows through the body/mind/spirit continuum. It can twist and turn and take many forms. And the way we discover our connection to the Universe and discover what our gifts are can also be serpentine and circuitous (even if what we'd like would be an easy, methodical, step-by-step set of directions). The way to connect with the energy of the Universe and to discover your gifts is just to get on the boat and begin wherever you begin.

You may find yourself drawn to one chapter or another; that's fine, just dive in and see where it takes you. If you read right through the book, you may notice that there's some repetition here and there; that's because the same idea or experience can be used or seen different ways in different contexts—the stream circles around and comes back on itself at times. You may become aware of different gifts in yourself at different times or you may find a pattern predominating; just see where they take you.

Chapter 1 will cover the two general ways people connect to the Universe. As I said, there are infinite ways, but they seem to fall into two general groups: those who see and those who feel. Seeing or feeling seems to be the first step, the first way of connecting.

Bon voyage. I hope you have a great journey listening to these voices and to the voices that come from beyond the other side of the couch.

Seeing or Feeling

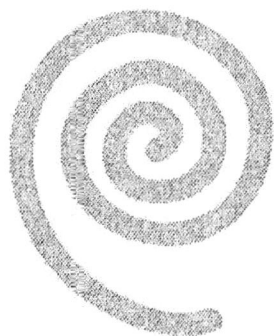

Seeing or Feeling

When people come into my office, I try to help them in several ways, perhaps through acupuncture or counseling, perhaps through helping them see where their pain comes from. One of the main ways I, as a shaman, can help, however, is not just to look at their distress, but also in a positive way to help them discover (a) their own individual gifts, (b) their power, and (c) their way of connecting to the energy of the Universe.

The traditional definition of a shaman is one who mediates between the physical world and other worlds. What other worlds? Who knows what all of the other realms are. As I sat with one woman who was unsure of where she was going in her life, she suddenly saw herself in a dark cave, black and sticky, but through the opening, she could see a sunlit beach. As she looked, I could see what she saw and let her know that I was there in case she needed help.

A shaman can move energy, talk to souls, get information. Many shamans will do the work for you; they will journey to other worlds for you and find whatever energy, information, or change you need. I prefer to make it a joint experience. I like to get you to journey into the other realms with me, to share what you find, and to make it a healing journey for you. This way I can help you learn how to connect with the energy of the Universe in your own way, and thus discover your own power and the individual gifts through which you express your power.

From the Power of the Universe to Our Gifts

Looking at this in a top down way, the key is to connect to the power of the Universe. You may call this the power of the Universe, god, energy, creative spirit, or anything else. It doesn't matter so long as you connect to it in the way that best fits who you are.

What does it mean, to connect to the Universe? That's hard to explain because it's a mystical experience, and a mystical experience is by definition something that can't be put into words. Taoists say that the way that can be spoken of is not the Way, the name that can be named is not the Name. You just feel the presence of the power of the Universe, feel it flowing through you. Some have tried to convey the experience: Ezekiel's vision of God, Buddha under the Bo tree losing his sense of self as a separate being, the dove descending to Jesus, Dante's ecstatic vision of being in the presence of God as love, healers who talk of God's power coming through them, the sense of unity in the Kama Sutra. Even an athlete who is in "the zone" or a writer or performer who loses all sense of self while creating is part of that flow of energy.

When you open to the power in the Universe, this energy flows through you and is manifested as your gifts. Think of the power of the Universe as analogous to electricity. You plug into it, it gives you power, and then you can use that power in the way that best fits your gifts.

Your gifts are the way the Universe's power is expressed in the physical world. You may have talent as a writer, a singer, a mathematician, a healer, or a shaman.

Hildegard de Bingen wrote that "[a]ll living creatures are, so to speak, sparks from the radiation of God's brilliance, and these sparks emerge from God like the rays of the sun.... For there is no creature without some kind of radiance—whether it be greenness, seeds, buds, or another kind of beauty" (4.11).

Lurianic Kabbalah, in an idea also explained by Adin Steinsaltz, says that when the vessel shattered, the shards (sparks) were scattered. When each person is born, he or she possesses one or more of these divine sparks. Each shard is necessary to tikun olam (repair of the world), just as the repair of any vessel requires all the parts. So it's important for each of us to value our own gifts and always look within others to help bring out their divine sparks.

Whatever your gift, this talent can be fully developed and work best only if the Universe's creative power gives it energy. If you try to push the talent without this connection, if you try to use just your own energy, you may well burn out or get sick. A radio's batteries will run out, but if it's plugged into a socket with access to unlimited energy, it can keep going. Think, for example, of the way some people say that praying (connecting to God) or meditating (absorption into the universe) enables them to keep doing good work in the hardest circumstances when others get burnt out.

From Our Gifts to the Power of the Universe

Now let's look at the same dynamic in a bottom-up kind of way, starting with our individual gifts and seeing how they connect us back to the Universe. We discover our gifts, then we find a power behind the gift, then find that this power comes from God, the Universe, the creative energy, a force which is huge, limitless, indefinable, but powerfully present. Someone as a child may doodle all the time or may find that he can draw better than his friends. As he grows older, he may take up painting seriously, work to develop his talent and not just draw for fun. Then after training and practice, he may find himself so absorbed in his work that he loses all sense of time and space, just working with complete absorption. The last step would be for him to realize that the inspiration isn't just his genius but something coming through him—and to find ways to let this energy flow through him.

Whatever your gift, it is as valid as anyone else's. It's your way. You may think you're strange or different. Other people may do things differently. You may feel inadequate because someone else can see auras and you can't. But each gift is good because it connects you to the Universe. What counts is that you come to know who you are and how you function best. You may not see auras, but you may feel someone else's emotions or be able to see quickly how a machine works.

How Can We Connect to the Power of the Universe?

Okay, so there are individual gifts and there is the power of the Universe. Now you may ask, "How do I go about connecting to the power of the Universe in order to use my gifts in the best way?"

Let me begin by using my own experience as an example of the indirectness of discovery. I started out doing martial arts and playing football. Clearly, I was a Warrior, but at that point I just thought I was a very strong athlete. I gained experience with Zen's discipline, focus, and search for non-self, realized I was a healer by practicing acupuncture, and then trained with a shaman. Finally, I came to understand that my healing gifts involved a power to see: when I worked with clients, I would first focus on their problems with my mind, then my aura would expand, and then I could see what was going on in them or around them.

When this happened, I would pause and try to be open to what the Universe (or God, or what you want to call it) moved me to do. This seeing thus enabled me to experience the power of the Universe, which would then help me act with my Warrior gift; I might clear away darkness, protect against dangers, see a client's strength, or accompany him or her on the journey toward healing.

I used to find out what people's gifts were and then work up the chain to help them learn how to connect to power. Now I try first to understand the process by which they connect to power. I happen to use seeing, but in fact there seem to be two main ways: through seeing or through feeling. All of the various ways that I've encountered seem to group under one of these two general categories. Both ways are inherent in all of us, but we tend to connect most strongly and most of the time in one way or the other.

Think about how you send or receive energy, or think about how you connect to your source of power. When you come into a new situation, what's the first thing you do? Do you see quickly what's going on with another person or do you need to get to know someone before you can make a connection? Can you tell by just looking at another person that he's had a bad day or do you gradually feel deeper and deeper layers of another person's situation or needs? You may not even be aware of what you do because you just assume that this is the way people work. You may even be impatient with or confused by others who seem unable to grasp what you do.

We can analyze this intellectually by stating that there are two major ways to connect to your power: one is dark, cold, concentrative, focused on third-eye seeing; the other is light, warm, and encompassing, centered on heart feeling. Remember, both approaches are fine, one isn't better than the other. They're just different. Again, all of us have it within us to do either one, but you will find you tend to do one or the other best or most naturally.

People Who Feel

Feeling people come from their hearts. They make a slower type of connection with others, and they are slower to move to their particular gift. Such people work the edges, building foundations and networking. Through gradually feeling out or sensing another person or being, they can gain a feeling of safety, and for feeling/heart people a sense of safety must come first. Then they can develop a feeling of connectedness with the other person. When this happens, they can intuit the other person's *feeling*, or a space opens up and they can step into this space, which allows them to feel what the other is experiencing or needs. Then they can use their power to help, or more accurately, let the power come through them to help in whatever way their gift takes them.

A yin feeler is someone who is quiet and withdrawn. Such a person is likely to sit quietly, waiting until he or she feels out what is going on. A yang feeler is more outgoing and expressive, likely to be sociable and to gather people together.

Of course there is a danger to any kind of shamanic work. The danger for the feeling/heart person is getting overwhelmed. Since people who work this way must have a heart connection before they can access their power, they run the risk of being too open emotionally and can thus get hurt or feel bombarded by the other person's emotions.

People Who See

The seeing, concentrative person comes from the third eye. This is a fast, cold, and clear process. It happens quickly, and there is no need first to build an emotional connection from the heart. The connection happens through hyper-concentration from the third eye. Seeing does not mean just using the physical eye and optic nerves. It encompasses physical sight, visions, thinking, hyperfocus, and the third eye. We're stuck for words and so use the term "seeing," but don't limit the meaning to physically seeing. Such a person may get a quick image of the other person's energy or of a force acting on the person. For example, such a person may see another's fear as a spiky ball or may see a spirit hovering near or may cut through a lot of talk to get to the central point. (Hemingway called this latter having a bullshit detector.) Once the seeing person gets this keen insight, he or she can let the power come through to act.

Because concentrative people tend to be fast, they may become impatient with people who come from the heart. They may also be susceptible to the danger of becoming arrogant or puffed up with ego. In order for others to be able to relate to them, and in order to do deep healing, they have to bring what they see to the heart, to feel, and then to act out of love.

You must remember that the kind of seeing or feeling that I'm talking about here has nothing to do with your intellect or with the way you cognitively process things. This is the process through which you use your personal power and connect with power, not the way you think with your brain. It's the way in which the Universe flows through you.

What Blocks Us from Using Our Power?

So we have different ways of using our powers. But we often have a hard time knowing what our gifts are or making a connection to our power or connecting to the power in the Universe. Or even believing that we have gifts or power. What keeps us from connecting? The obvious answer is fear. Fear of what? My experience of looking at myself and from working with many people is that we are afraid of our power and of the power of the Universe flowing through us. Strange, you might say. If we have gifts, why don't we just use them?

One explanation is that when people are young and they do use their gifts, they may feel different from those around them, they may feel unlike others in their families, or they may feel like outsiders at school. Parents may criticize them or try to make them fit into the family's ways. Teachers may not understand that the quiet boy sitting there and saying nothing is actually sensing the nature of those around him or that the girl who gets angry with others doesn't understand they can't see what she does. One person I know with concentrative power, for example, was told from a young age that she was intellectually bright; since the family was academically inclined, they just pushed her to do well in school, so she didn't understand she was using a deeper kind of intuition and felt like a failure if she didn't get all As. Or someone else, who had a heart gift, was told she wasn't smart because she wasn't good at math even though she had brilliant insight into others. Such children may be hurt or ridiculed. They may get into trouble with parents or teachers. Or they may simply feel alone or "weird." They have no context to understand or use their gifts.

Such a sense of being different forces people to build very strong barriers or defense mechanisms against using the gifts consciously. After all, other people don't see them as strengths or may laugh at us or put pressure on us to conform. Children try to fit into what they learn is the ordinary way of being. A heart person, for example, may protect herself from accusations of being stupid by learning to be quiet, to disappear so she won't be noticed and criticized. Years later, when she begins to use the gift again, these defenses come up again strongly, and she feels afraid she'll again be criticized or feel like an outsider—so she hides again. The very thing you developed to protect yourself, the defense that in fact may have helped you survive in the world as a child, now prevents you from being aware of, valuing, and using your gift.

When I asked a man why he didn't use his gift of feeling with and loving others, he said, "because I'm afraid of failing." Everyone says that, so I asked, "What does that mean?" He replied, "I don't want to be disappointed in myself or to hurt anyone else." Again I asked, "What does that mean?" He got to the heart of the matter when he realized "When I was growing up, everyone was trying to form me into what was out there. When I couldn't play as roughly or as skillfully as the other boys, I was called stupid and sissy. I was afraid that if people noticed me, they'd see I was incompetent, so I just sort of tried to make myself invisible at school, and didn't say much at home either." Now this man is a promising healer because he can use his gift of gently connecting to others.

A woman who had always seen herself as obliging and giving had a terrifying vision of Siva the destroyer. As she sat with it, he told her that she was his daughter, a strong Warrior. This woman had grown up learning to act dependent because that's the way women were supposed to be. She had feared that if she acted powerful and direct, she wouldn't be loved. So each time she started to assert herself, she would get afraid and squelch the impulse; she would become reactive rather than assertive, trying to sense what others wanted rather than feeling what she really felt. Now she is learning to bring up her power and cut right through problems.

Once you understand and can bear the fear, you can find your gift and use it.

Still, connecting to the universe is literally awesome and overwhelming. Being in the presence of unlimited greatness is very scary. One person told of the first time he experienced God. He was walking with his elderly, sick dog and trying to think of ways to help her when "suddenly it felt as if the top of my head cracked open. I connected to a magnitude of power that is limitless. It was terrifying. Then I said, 'ok I'll stay with the fear.' Now when I do my healing work, I try to connect with God to help me discern my clients' trouble and to help me work with them to heal."

Connecting to the power of the Universe is frightening because you can lose the feeling of being you or of being a self. The ego is used to being in control and defining who we are. In this case, it is overpowered by the big Self, as it were. We identify ourselves with our ego, and when this is gone, when there is just Being, who are we? Ordinarily, I can think of myself as a parent, a teacher, a taxpayer, someone who has these particular memories and those particular abilities. But when the power of the universe is doing the feeling, the acting, we disappear.

Yet a third fear of using our power is fear that we may get overwhelmed by others. And indeed, if I attach to the power as being my power, then the needs, demands, or methods of others may overwhelm me. Or others may feed on our power and diminish it or make us move away from the true source of the power.

One person explained that when she's alone, meditating, feeling the power come through her to see and act as a shaman, she's fine. However, when she comes back to the world, people attach to her because they are attracted to her power and want some of it. They want her to love them or to take care of them or to make them feel strong. She sees this and then goes out of the larger power and gives some of her power to them by giving them what they want rather than seeing for herself what is best. Or she may get confused and think they can do better at something that she can do well enough herself, so she lets them tell her how to run a meeting or how to organize her business. She said, "If I stayed in my power, I'd realize what was happening and not give away my power. The key is learning to be in my power by staying connected to the infinite power."

Fear can block us from using our power in yet a fourth way. If we are afraid of our power, every time we try to use it or access it, people around us feel the fear not the power. Because we see them pull away, we then build the belief that our power will hurt or harm others or repel them. What they are really reacting to, however, is our fear of the power, not the power itself. When a student in my sword class looked for a partner to spar with, people edged away. He thought they were worried that he was so strong and agile. In fact he was, but others who were even stronger had no trouble getting sparring partners. What was going on was that he was afraid he'd not be able to control his power, and his classmates sensed that he was afraid of his strength. Once you can overcome the fear, you will find that people will be drawn to your power, not put off by it.

Fear is an unpleasant feeling, so to speak, a scary feeling. But if you can simply notice that it's there and let yourself feel it, you'll realize it's just an emotion. You can learn a lot just by watching, and even have fun with the feeling. Say to yourself, "Whoops, here's the fear, what triggered that?" Or you might notice that your feeling shy is an attempt to feel safe and then explore what might have caused that desire to disappear. You won't be destroyed by an emotion; you'll actually feel more whole and real if you let yourself feel the fear. Then, like other feelings, it will make a bow and pass along. Just as we can watch a cloud pass through the sky, we can observe the way an emotion feels and moves. Maybe it will come back from time to time, but just notice again, and gradually, it will go on its way.

We can move beyond fear to realize we are powerful as seers or feelers. In this chapter, I've tried to explain these two general ways of responding to ordinary reality and of connecting to the Universe. Some of the specific patterns described in the following chapters may be more likely to occur in seers, some may be more likely in feelers, and some just take different forms depending on whether a person's basic mode is seeing or feeling. Again, remember there aren't any rules or value judgments; all are just modes of being. We are who we are.

Patterns

Calling the Souls

This is one of the most basic and most common patterns in the traditions I have learned. A person can call the souls, or a soul may just appear to the person without the person's having consciously called it. People gifted with this pattern may be seers or feelers, and they may come into contact with the souls in a variety of ways. The soul may come in a dream or simply appear to a person who is awake. Or the person may chant, drum, use psychotropic plants, channel, or just call the soul to come.

One purpose of connecting with a soul may be to help the soul move on. A soul may need to have help in moving toward the light, or a soul may need to communicate with someone he or she loves to feel at peace or to comfort or help the loved one. Also, one can gain information and guidance from a soul. For example, a woman who had to make a decision about an operation was visited by the soul of her father, who had been a physician before he died; he told her what he thought the procedure should involve and warned her against more radical versions.

Another person I worked with, named Eli, is an example of someone who calls the souls. When I met him, he was a rabbinical student. Rabbinical study involves close and extended study of

Hebrew texts, so I first expected him to be a seer, maybe a hyper-focusing person. But he turned out to be a yang feeler.

What would happen was that Eli would be studying a text very intensely, and he would connect to the soul of the author or to the soul of a figure in the text. Eli would call the soul to him, then his heart would open, and he would go to a clear space out of linear time. At that point, the room where he was studying and his text would disappear.

This happened, for example, when Eli was in a class studying a puzzling passage in Genesis about the Patriarch Abraham, who could be puzzling indeed. There are often ambiguities in Jewish texts, so one thing students do is try to figure out sound interpretations. As he was concentrating, Eli moved into the clear space and then found himself sitting in a classroom different from the one in which he had been bodily sitting with the other students. Abraham himself was there, standing at the front of the room and speaking the words of the text. Eli then asked Abraham what he meant in that particular passage, and Abraham answered.

When Eli came back to the physical world, he remembered what Abraham had said. He looked around—all his fellow students were there, and his rabbi was asking for interpretations. The rabbi called on Eli, who then gave the interpretation of the text as Abraham had explained it. The rabbi was impressed and asked where Eli had gotten this understanding from. As Eli asked me later, "What are you going to say?"

One of the most gifted people at calling the souls I have ever known was a seer named Aingeal. This is her story about the first time she worked with me to call the souls.

"The truth is I didn't go see John because I wanted therapy. I went to see him because I needed help. Someone or something was tormenting me.

"In June of '03, a friend of my husband visited us from Atlanta. Shortly after he left, I started to have nightmares, or something like nightmares. I would wake up every night in complete and utter horror. I would wake up feeling that my body weighed a ton.

"I couldn't move my arms or legs, and I had no voice. I would try to scream and would slap or kick my husband to wake him up, but my arms and legs wouldn't move, and strange noises would come out of my mouth.

"I would wake up and see this man standing over my bed staring at me. He was very tall and thin, and he wore a naval uniform. He wouldn't say anything. He would just stare at me. When I would finally gain some control over my body, I would wake my husband up crying, and glue myself to him for the rest of the night. I hadn't felt so much fear since I was a little girl, when my parents would find me sleeping on their bedroom floor. Eventually I outgrew that and forgot about it until this new experience. I didn't outgrow this one though.

"The man kept coming every night, but it wasn't until I started to see him during the day that I totally freaked out. One day I was sitting on my bed getting dressed when my son, who was nine years old then, walked in and said, 'That's weird. I just saw someone standing over your bed.' Need I say more? My husband took the kids out that day to give me a break, and I spent the whole time sitting outside talking to my best friend on the phone because I was too afraid to be alone in my house. That was clearly a sign I needed help.

"So that Monday I went to see John for the first time. I told him what was happening and he said, 'So why don't you just ask him what he wants?' Gee why didn't I think of that? A ghost has been haunting me and I should just talk with him. No way. Who's the crazy one here exactly? Still, I liked John and there was something about him that made me decide not to dismiss him as a quack and hear him out.

"John said I had the gift of seeing (yeah, right, you call this a gift?). He told me the man was harmless, and once I acknowledged him, he would go away. By the time the hour was up I felt better. Not because I had a recipe to get rid of the haunting, but because John didn't put a straight jacket on me and send me to a mental institution. I'd had flashes while driving to see him that while I was telling him about the 'thing,' he would smile and say something like 'Hhhmm..., so let me make sure I understand you. You see a man standing over your bed at night and now during the day? Hhhmmm...and how long has this been going on?' And as he sweet talked me and made me feel as if he was going to make it all better, he would slowly press this red button under his desk and all these people with white coats would come running into the room and start strapping me down. I had seen things many times in the past but I never dared to talk about it with anyone because I was sure I'd end up in a padded room with people sliding food to me from a small slot under my door.

"Luckily John didn't have any red buttons under his desk; for that matter, he didn't even sit behind a desk. He sat on a big black leather chair that might as well have been a recliner because he was so laid back into it. He was so confident that if I just asked the man what he wanted, the man would go away. John was so convincing that I even almost believed him.

"It took a few more horrifying nights before I finally decided to take John's advice. So one night after being woken up for the 57th thousandth time by the man, I built the strength to mumble something like, 'Who are you?' I know I screwed up because John had told me to ask him what he wanted not who he was, but that's what came out. Strangely enough, I heard the man say, 'Dan-lee.'

I thought I heard him wrong, so I paid closer attention, and sure enough, he said 'Dan-lee' again. He said, 'Dan-lee' about fifty more times until I said, 'OK I got it. Your name is Dan-lee.' Great, I finally built the strength to talk to my tormentor and he probably doesn't even speak English with a name like that.

"Well, Dan-lee stuck around for a while, but surprisingly I wasn't afraid of him anymore. With time I was able to see him more and more clearly. I would see his face and his uniform in detail, and even though I didn't know anything but his name, I realized John was right. He was harmless.

"A few months later my husband's friend from Atlanta asked him to be his best man. So the three of us hopped on a plane and headed off to be at Bill's wedding. There were three of us because Dan-lee tagged along, and he seemed more eager than anyone to go.

"The day after we got there, my husband brought me to meet Bill's mother. She was a sweet woman in her fifties, with a beautiful heart you could see through her eyes and so much pain that shadowed those beautiful eyes. Within a matter of seconds of my sitting next to her, she told me her life story. She talked about her husband a lot. He had died ten years before from a sudden heart attack.

"As she talked about him, she went through her purse and pulled out a wedding picture of her and ...'Dan-lee!' I said out loud when I saw the picture of the groom. There was my Dan-lee in his uniform standing next to this woman some thirty years ago. Same body, same face, even same uniform.

"She looked at me and said, 'What did you say?' I was in complete and total shock. I couldn't even speak. I mumbled something like, 'He looks like someone I've been dreaming about for the last few months, someone who keeps saying his name is Dan-lee.'"

"Her eyes became so wide, and they filled with tears as she stared at me with this very strange expression on her face. I couldn't believe what I had just said to this poor woman who was obviously still mourning the loss of her husband. Idiot! She's going to think I escaped from a mental institution to go crash her son's wedding. As I was struggling in my head to think of what I was going to say to make up for my stupidity, she said,

"'Danny Lee.' "Excuse me? What did she just say? Then she said it again.

"'Danny Lee. That's what I used to call my husband. His real name is Robert Daniel Lee, but only I called him Danny Lee. You saw my Danny Lee? How is he? What did he say? Why did he leave me like that so suddenly?'

"As she asked me about her husband, she cried as if he had died just yesterday. I looked over and saw Dan-lee standing next to her with one hand on her shoulder trying to comfort her, but he too was crying. He was crying with her and for her. It was beautiful and sad at the same time. I couldn't answer questions because by then I was crying, no, sobbing too. She hugged me and said, 'You must be a very good person with a good heart if you can see my Danny Lee.'

"I know I helped Dan-lee connect with his wife, and I know it's something he's wanted to do for many years, and I know she felt connected with her husband at that moment. I knew she could sense his presence while we hugged and cried, and I know it was the first time in ten years that she didn't feel so alone. I felt honored. Honored to be part of that moment. I have never felt so much love in my entire life, so much love that my chest felt like it was going to explode. At that moment, at that second nothing existed around me except for this couple and their unconditional love for each other. No pain, no past, no sadness, no fears for myself, nothing else. The only thing that was real at that moment was this incredibly contagious, overwhelming feeling of love; and even though it didn't belong to me, I felt privileged to finally see and feel the true meaning of 'unconditional love.'

"Dan-lee got to tell his wife that he still loves her and that he is watching over her. He got to tell her that he's not gone and he's there for her. His wife got to tell him she was angry and hurt that he left her, sad and alone, feelings that had been holding her back for so many years. She had the opportunity to tell him how much she loved him and missed him."

Aingeal's gift is that she has the ability to "see" the souls she is calling. Sometimes they come unbidden and then it is her role to give information to people. Once this happens, the soul will move on and leave Aingeal. Sometimes she will actually try to seek and call on a specific soul if she sees that someone needs the contact.

Other people may channel the information from the souls—they can either "talk" with them or are possessed by them to deliver the message. Edgar Casey is an example of the latter.

Aingeal realized that she had seen the ghost and then had somehow brought him to his wife. Her seeing had allowed her to tap into her power and make possible the loving meeting of these two beings.

How does that happen?

Seeing itself doesn't give access to one's own power or to the Universal power. But to see does take awareness and energy. The energy which comes up when Aingeal or anyone else sees is part of the universal energy. This seeing becomes rather like a suction, it starts a flow. She can attach to that flow, in her case, a flow of dark energy (that's the way universal energy flows through her). If she can attach to the flow she can use it beneficially. That's what she did with Dan-lee and his wife even though at the time she wasn't fully aware of what she was doing.

Since this experience, Aingeal has been learning to recognize she doesn't just have passive visions; she can deliberately use what she sees to help herself and other people. She can learn to call the souls, to invite the process actively. Depending on what she sees and what the universe tells her it means, she may warn someone of something, or help a person see what she (Aingeal) does, or interpret for someone why he has been having the troubles he has, or comfort someone who's puzzled. She can use her magnificent gift to help others along their ways.

Possession

I met Ian on a fine spring day, 35 degrees with clear blue sky and a 20 mph wind—just how I like it. His major complaint was that he had not felt like himself since he was in a car accident ten years before. Ian said he felt possessed. People come and see me all the time telling me they are possessed by something or someone is trying to hurt them. Rarely does it prove to be a true possession. Usually it is some other personal issue or a separation that needs to be addressed.

Originally from Colorado, Ian was around forty years old and worked as a lawyer in Boston. Both his parents had been killed in a car accident when he was a baby. He was brought up and adopted by an aunt by marriage. She'd never had children and her husband had died a year before she adopted Ian.

Ian's time with his aunt was not pleasant. She told him he never did anything right, and when she got angry, she would whip him with a belt. Moreover, she never protected him from a man who abused him. After high school, he left and never looked back. He came to Boston to law school and then took a job with a small firm. One night he was at a party that went late into the night. He was tired when he left to drive home but had not been drinking. He lost control of the car, went off the road, and hit an embankment. He describes it:

"It was my fault for not wearing a seat belt—when I hit the embankment, my head smashed into the windshield. First I felt severe pain, and then nothing. I felt as if I were floating above the accident scene, like the descriptions I've read of near-death experiences, and looked down and saw myself in the car. It felt as if I were rising up and away. But then I saw my aunt. She looked shadowed, her eyes cruel and her mouth tight and angry. She said, 'You are not going to get away so easily.' I heard her laugh and then was back in my body in the car.

"There was a fireman in the car with me trying to free me from behind the wheel. The pain was so intense, I passed out and knew nothing else until I regained consciousness in the hospital several days later."

Ian had severe head injuries, a broken leg and arm, plus other injuries. He was told he was lucky to be alive.

He went on, "I never felt like myself after that. I was always tired, felt detached at work, and had no affect when talking with colleagues and friends. I can work in an analytical, logical way, but I think that my clients are bothered by my disengagement.

"The doctors say this change resulted from my head injuries, but I'm not sure that explains everything. This sounds strange, but since I saw my aunt at the accident, she seems to have changed. Before that, her health had been bad, with breathing difficulties and angina. But after the accident she got much better. It's almost as if she gained power as I lost it. Is that idea totally far-fetched? I'm here partly because a friend told me you were open to such possibilities."

As I looked around Ian, I could not find him. First, he appeared to me as a shell, empty with no soul. It felt very cold and dark. I could find his aunt. She seemed all over him, entwined, with no space between them. I could see her like an overlay on him; she was in her fifties, with black hair, strong features, and wearing a blue, almost turquoise dress. Her hands were coming out at me like the claws of a hermit crab, and her whole demeanor was very aggressive toward me. I could see Ian under her, almost like seeing someone underwater. Then the image shifted and he seemed off to the side because she was so dominant. Ian is sitting there talking to me, but I'm seeing the aunt. At this point, a cold dark feeling came over me and I knew what he said was true. He was possessed.

Possession is rare because usually when something attaches to a person, the person is still himself and can be seen and felt as present. He may be drained or bombarded, but he is still there. With possession, however, something comes in and takes over. What happens to the person? There are three main possibilities: (1) the person dies and something possesses his body, or (2) the possessor buries the original person so he doesn't have control anymore, or (3) it moves the original person outside the body. In this latter case, there's a person in front of me and there's another off to the side. In some cases, it's the possessor off to the side, but in Ian's case, the original soul was off to the side, rather like being in storage.

There are degrees and gradations, from hearing yourself saying something in your mother's voice to total possession; with total possession, the person possessed speaks, acts, and values things as the possessor does. In each case, though, the people are lifeless, dull, not there. When I look, I can't see a separation between the person and what is possessing her. I may get different images of the same person on different days; it's fluid, for what I get on a particular day is what I need to work with on that day.

The person who is possessed may be in the room, talking and responding, but she isn't there; I can't find her. We've all had the experience of talking with someone who seems to disappear from the conversation. Possession is like that but permanent. It's different from merely being distracted. When you're distracted or daydreaming, in a way you're not there, but you know where you are or can snap yourself back to where you are.

The next question might be "Why does possession happen?" Most commonly it's to gain power or energy. The being steals your energy.

Why do some people get possessed? What makes them susceptible? There are two main ways: (1) through trauma, as in Ian's case. The trauma made him weak and thus he let his aunt in. She'd been lying in wait for a vulnerable moment. Remember what she said, "You are not going to get off so easily," (2) through a parent's or guardian's being overly domineering. We're always susceptible to parents anyway, so one who goes beyond the limits of love can subsume a child and take over control of his being. Both factors were present for Ian.

I think Ian was dying that night he crashed, but somehow before he actually died, his aunt came and took over his soul. She did this so she could use his energy, so she could live and be stronger. She did this because she felt she was owed his life since she had brought him up.

I asked myself, was he still alive? The problem was that I was not sure where he was. Obviously he was sitting in front of me physically. What I was concerned about was the location of his soul. As we moved his aunt away from him, what was going to replace her? Was he still there but overlaid by his aunt, or had he really died? What would happen if I separated him from his aunt? Would he die? What would happen?

In the end, it turned out that in order to survive, his soul had just left. It was partially there, but had left and was waiting to come back. If he had been totally possessed, he wouldn't have come to see me; there was a battle between him and his aunt because he was trying to get control back. Even though I was unsure at the time, I thought the challenge was how to get him back into his body. To do this, there was work Ian had to do and there was work I had to do.

When I began working with Ian, he could neither see nor feel, so I could not begin with him by helping him see or feel more consciously. I did not want to frighten him, but I knew and he instinctively knew that something had happened with his aunt after the accident. So I began by describing how to do a separation with him. There are many bonds that connect us to those in our life. To me they look like thin white threads or roots. There can be many of them connecting us to another person or just a single one, depending on the relationship with that person. One of the first things I learned when I began this work was how to help people separate from another person. You want to do this so the karma between you and that person (alive or not) is ended and so the energy that passes between you is ended.

I can usually do the separation myself, but I have found it is very valuable for people to take part in their own healing. This being the case, I began with having Ian work on separating because it was the only thing he might be capable of doing. Since his aunt was occupying the same body with him, I knew that in the beginning this slight separation wouldn't be enough to get rid of her, but once we moved her away from him a little, I could see her and see him with a little distance between them; then we could work on taking out the roots one by one.

I started by having Ian focus his anger on his aunt. He could do this in any way he wanted, by writing, talking, or imagining. We began this way so that he could get in touch with his rage toward her and so that he could access the power of his rage. I hoped that in this way he could use his feeling to begin pulling his soul back into his body. Anger could help him feel, and he then could bring the feeling into my room and thus feel present to me and to himself.

Feeling was very scary for Ian, and at first he did not do any of the anger work I had asked him to do.

"Did you try?" I asked.

"Yes, but I couldn't do the work at all. Every time I summoned up her image, what you term calling her soul, I was overwhelmed by so much fear, I couldn't continue."

"Remember we talked about being in your body?" I asked.

"Yes," he said.

"Your body is not a safe place to be right now," I said. "All the memories of the pain you suffered in the accident will come back. In addition, the memory of your aunt will come back too. You're asking yourself, 'Why should I come back at all if this is what I am going to feel?' A reasonable question, but I do not know any other way for you to be happy. When you are not present or aware, you feel safe. The truth of the matter is that your body is always absorbing the energy around you, in this case, your aunt's, and if you are not aware of what is happening, you will continue to suffer. At this point happiness is a long way off."

"I understand, but it is very scary all the same," Ian replied. "There's huge fear and the prediction of a return of pain, but no clear benefit at least that I can feel now. It seems like a never-ending process with no light at the end of the tunnel."

"It is a long process wading through the swamp of your being. But the more you practice awareness, the easier it gets."

This was even harder than it sounds. The body was a scary place for Ian. It never felt safe when he was growing up, and he had spent the last few years not very present. The safest and easiest way to get someone back into his body is to get him to feel an emotion. So working with his rage toward his aunt was a good beginning.

One day, several sessions later, Ian said, "You know it is really strange, I thought sending anger to my aunt as you have me doing was a waste of time. But, I said to myself, John seems to know what he is doing, so why not try it. As I pushed through my fear, the rage really began to take over. When I would call on her, the energy was so strong I felt as though I could easily kill her. I literally shook with the emotion."

"Now how do you feel?" I asked.

"This is the really strange part," Ian replied. "The rage is beginning to fade; I cannot call it up with anything like the power I once did."

"As the rage dissipates, you need to replace it with love. The rage works to get you to feel and to direct your anger toward your aunt. However, rage will never heal. Only love can heal. As the rage disappears, you will find the image of your aunt will also begin to fade. At this time I want you to begin sending her feelings of love and compassion."

"Why would I do that, after all she has done to me?"

"You are not doing this for her," I explained. "You are doing this for you. It is only with love that you can heal. You must let her go with love so she has no attachment to you anymore. In this way the karma between you is released and you are both free to go your own ways."

It is a process that will take lots of time. I have to convince Ian it is worth his while to stay in the here and now. That means he will feel both emotionally and physically. He will feel how his body feels, and after the accident there is a lot of pain he has not been aware of.

To sum up, he needs to harness the rage to give himself power. He sends the rage to her and has to learn to want and act to love himself and then, finally, needs to send love to her. Over time, the roots of connection will gradually untangle.

If he is able to make it this far, the final step will be for him to connect to the Universe.

While Ian was doing his work to feel, I was also working to have his aunt detach from him. The separation wouldn't work unless both our parts were going on.

I had to proceed slowly. I had no idea what would happen if I sent her away. Was he still there just underneath her? Since this was not a loving situation, I called on Ian's aunt and showed myself in a dark form. I have the ability to show up in the other realms in many different forms. People see me in different ways, maybe a Warrior, maybe a bear, maybe a demon, but I don't see myself as anything, I just show up. It does not matter the form I take because it is the dark power behind me that is important. I usually choose a very dark Warrior power for this type of work. In this situation, my bringing love won't get rid of the possessor; it will just get absorbed.

His aunt noticed me right away. I would have been surprised if she hadn't. She did not want to let go. This was a free meal. On the other hand, she was very much afraid of me.

I wanted to be careful because I had no idea what was going to happen to Ian and I had no idea what would happen to her. So I began by talking to her and scaring her, seeing if I could get her to let go on her own. I call this the bargaining stage, saying "either you go or you're going to be made to go." I will do this once then back it up with power. I use the power by directing my attention to what is needed in the other realms. I then wait and see what I am called to do. I do this so my ego is not involved in making a decision. If the powers around me want me to, I am directed to act on Ian's behalf. Since she was not going to leave on her own and I was directed to act, I began the process.

I was called to create a black hole-like thing behind her and open it up to another universe. I created a connection between the black hole and Ian's aunt. I then began to move her with the power toward the black hole. The hole also began pulling her like a powerful suction. This will over time tire her out and she will not be able to hold onto Ian. It is important for me to do this slowly so she lets go of her own accord. This is important so there will not be any roots left in Ian. It is like pulling up a weed; you have to get all the roots so the weed will not grow back. Or to use another image, it's like a crane, which is pulling up a tree stump: the crane pulls like the black hole, and I am, or rather the power is, digging up the roots. It can be a slow process.

If the aunt goes and if Ian can feel his body and regain his soul, then we can try to find out whether he sees or feels as his way to connect to the Universe. I suspect he will turn out to be a feeler because he was captured so easily. Once he connects, he will, like others, feel increasing power, calm, and development of his gifts.

Love Heals

Carin sat in our Way of Power training group for four weeks before she said anything except to introduce herself in a very soft voice. When we met one-on-one, she was shy and self-depre-cating. I'd invited her to join the group because I thought she had the unusual potential to be a Loving Healer, but she would have none of it.

"Sure," she said, "I love my kids and my pets, but everyone does that."

The change started when she was upset about her cat. He was fourteen years old and suffering from serious heart trouble. He could barely walk across the room and was eating and drinking little, a bad sign that he was approaching the end. Pressing back into the cushions of the couch, Carin could hardly bear to talk about his pain and weakness.

"Well, why don't you heal him?" I asked.

"I'm willing to try to do whatever I can for him, but how in the world would I heal him?"

I wasn't going to give her specific directions because I wanted her to find her own power. And besides, since my gift is seeing more than feeling, I couldn't tell her how to be her own kind of feeler until she did it and I saw what she did. What I could do was try to help her in her own way, which in this case meant challenging her.

"Just go home and love him."

She looked dubious and laughed nervously.

The next time we met, three weeks later, she reported that she had been very unsure, didn't know what to say or do, but then figured she'd try what she'd done with her children when they were babies.

"I sat in my rocking chair, the one with soft blue cushions where I'd rocked my kids when they were little, took him on my lap and cradled him. I rocked and loved, loved and rocked. He tried to get away. 1 put him down and let him go. Later I picked him up again, and rocked and loved some more. Then I let him go again. He wanted to go back to his cushion by the stove and be alone.

"After a few days like this, on a sunny morning, when the light was gentle through the windows, I came into my room and he was lying by the rocker seeming to wait for me. I put him on my lap and again cradled him as I rocked. I told him that I loved him and wanted whatever was best for him. If he was ready to go, I would try to help him be comfortable. If he wanted to stay, I would just keep loving him and delight in his being."

Carin looked astonished. "Now, after just three weeks, all his symptoms are gone. He's eating and walking around like a stately elder. How did that happen?"

Like most feelers, Carin works intuitively and didn't know what she had done; she just did it. It took one more experience for her to be convinced that something special was going on.

She had gained a little more trust in the group and a bit of confidence from her experience with her cat. So she came into a meeting a month later and told us this story:

"I was sitting on my deck on a beautiful Sunday morning in May, enjoying the delicate green of the new leaves. I put my mug of tea down on the railing, and watched a dragonfly with iridescent blue wings circle the cup two or three times; she came lower and then to my distress landed in the mug. I stood up fast and looked into the mug; her wings fluttered and then she lay still.

"Afraid she had drowned, I reached in and lifted her out. She lay on my hand and didn't move, so I put her on the railing, hoping that would help. But she still didn't move. I felt terrible. I put her on my hand and told her the world would miss her. I told her I was sorry, I didn't mean for her to come to harm. I told her I loved her and hoped she would live and have lots of little dragonflies.

"Her wings started to move faintly and I talked to her some more. When her body shifted a bit, I put her on the railing, hoping the warmth of the sun would help. She began to right herself and her wings began to move more evenly, shining again with translucent color. After about five minutes, she flew away."

Now the others in the group told Carin that she had done something special. "But what?" she asked.

"Everyone can have some effect on another being," I explained.

"When we interact with others, both our energy and their energy changes. That's why lots of people can do Reiki and move energy a little. Your energy changed the dragonfly's energy. Think of acupuncture: when there's a blockage of energy or an excess of energy, acupuncture changes the flow of the person's energy.

"But you do something more, you go beyond what most people can do because you have a true gift of healing."

I asked Carin to tell me again what she had done with the cat and the dragonfly. As she went through the process, I was able to go with her, feel what she was feeling and see what it was she was doing. When I do this with people, I'm experiencing what they're doing, and I get a picture, like seeing on a film. Different shamans describe the journey differently; this is just how I take the journey with a feeler. After working with Carin and other people who can heal through love, I figured out some steps in the process.

The first step is connecting heart to heart. It feels like a physical connection, sort of like a tube of energy opening between the two people. The tube image is just one simile; sometimes it's like a hose, and sometimes it bends. Bushmen describe lines or ropes. It's rather like two countries on either side of a river with a bridge between them; you can feel each other's energy, but there's nothing crossing the bridge yet, nothing in the tube yet. Possibilities are present but nothing's happening yet.

The next step occurs if both people are willing. [This process works with animals too, as shown in Carin's story, but for simplicity, I'm going to use the word person.] The Healer's heart opens to the loving, healing energy coming from the universe. This loving energy from the universe comes down into the back heart chakra (remember that there are parallel chakra systems for each site, front and back), then through the front heart chakra to the other person. In healing, the energy goes in this one direction; this was the case with the cat and the dragonfly. But the best results come when the flow goes through the other person too; then the energy flows both ways, through both people, like a circle of energy.

Some healing can happen whenever two people open to the energy. But Carin can go beyond this stage. When the energy builds, she experiences a clear space, like the clear space one can reach in meditating. There's no thought, no nothing, one just is. Carin can go into this clear space that's beyond the original connection. Then she starts to ride a wave of love; love just flows through her. She felt a wave of love for the dragonfly; she didn't force it or compel it; it just flowed through her. Some people get a bit of this feeling when they hold a baby.

This loving energy changed the dragonfly's energy. Literally, the energy that was in the dragonfly and the cat altered. I don't know how it alters; it just does. That's the healing.

Now Carin is using her ability to heal people, and they seem to find their way to her as if sensing that she can help. For example, she worked on a man who had always been an aggressive athlete and was having considerable pain in his leg that kept him from even walking comfortably. As she worked on him, he became aware of a loving presence, a "blue lady," who counseled him to be gentle. His pain hasn't totally disappeared, but he is convinced that the blue lady is a figure guiding him to be more loving with himself and with others, and that doing so will help ease the pain and prevent further physical injury.

Carin still works intuitively and does not need to see what she's doing; in fact, trying to see or thinking too much might get in her way. My being able to see and articulate what's happening has merely given her some validation so she doesn't question herself so much; now she's actively putting herself in situations where others can find her, letting others know she does healing—and they're beginning to find her.

Different Healers may have different experiences of what they do although the underlying process is similar: conveying love. Allan, for example, also helped his pet. The small beagle would have seizures; he would convulse, his eyes would bulge, his tongue would hang out, and he would pant, sometimes lose control of his bowels or, most frightening, be unable to move at all. Allan described the turning point this way:

"One night I retired earlier than the rest of the family. I went into my bedroom, closed the door, turned off the lights, meditated for a short while, then got into bed and dozed off. A little while later, I was awakened by a commotion in the hall. When I opened the door, I saw my wife and daughter trying to help my dog, who was convulsing with an unusually violent seizure. Since I had been meditating earlier and still felt "in the space" [remember this from the description of Carin's ability to go into a clear space?], I thought I'd go back into the bedroom and try to go back into meditation and practice what little I knew about healing.

"As I was closing the door, I noticed what looked like a small stick figure or icon in the corner of the hallway. Wondering whether this was perhaps the ghost of a dog or a dog demon or something like that, as I began meditating, I tried to visualize it and talk to it. I told it that it had no place in this home, that we didn't need it here and that it should go away and leave my dog alone. I said that it could go safely, and then I felt the most loving connection with it.

"Almost immediately, my wife called that the seizure had suddenly ended. I told her confidently that there wouldn't be any more seizures and there haven't been."

Allan is a very loving, strongly built, forceful man in his fifties. His story shows how a Loving Healer can banish dark or negative energy with the use of love. First, he connected with his dog when the animal was in great pain. This connection opened Allan's heart chakra. Because the heart chakra was open, the energy of the universe flowed through it. Then, already clear because of having just meditated, he moved into a space where he could visualize what the darkness around his dog looked like. As he spoke to the darkness, he was able not to be afraid of it or harsh with it, but to become loving toward it. He was able to talk with and love the darkness until it dissolved. He had changed its energy, and that changed his dog's energy so it was healthy again.

Love can also help ease fear. Fear is a bully: if you fight it or sit on it, it becomes worse. If you love it, it dissipates. How does that work? We all feel fear and try to avoid it or situations that bring it up. The first step is to look at the fear and try to see what part of you is afraid. The mind can monitor and prepare the heart. For example, someone is afraid to go see a doctor because she's afraid of what the diagnosis will be. If she can step back and see where the fear is say, in her heart, and send it love, keep saying "I love you, I love you," the fear may ease and her heart may unclench.

Sometimes, though, it's just too scary to look at the fear, to let oneself feel it fully. Or the fear may be hidden and a person may not even be aware that fear is there. For example, sometimes when a person is angry, underneath the anger the real problem may be fear, but it feels stronger to yell at someone else than to admit that one feels powerless. After all, why do we get angry at a doctor who can't give us a cure?

One way that I as a shaman can help in such cases is to sense the other person's fear. If I can feel your fear, I feel it where you do. If it's in your heart or stomach, I'll feel it in my heart or stomach. If it's in your unconscious mind, I can try to locate it there. Then, once I sense where the fear is, I can tell that part of me that I love it, send it love, open myself to the universal energy to let love flow through that part of me. This will release the fear in me and then release it in you.

People feel safe with me because they know I'm not going to hurt them and because they trust that I won't let anything else hurt them. This is the Warrior in me. But increasingly, I'm realizing that healing comes through love. First I experience what's going on and then I try to open to love.

Healing through love is very wonderful, but of course there's also danger in this kind of spiritual activity, as in all others. The danger for Healers, and for feelers in general, is that they take on other people's stuff and literally absorb their energy. There's a paradox here: in order to be a Healer, you have to let yourself feel the other person's pain, and that means taking on some of their energy. Then the healer's aura starts to get dark with the accumulated suffering. The need of others is endless as anyone in the nursing, medical, teaching, social work, or ministerial fields knows. So the Healer can be harmed by the process of healing. How does a Healer or feeler protect himself or herself?

The key is awareness. You have to feel what others feel in order to help, but then you need to be clear on what's your own energy or feeling and what is not yours but is that of the other person, whose pain or fear or illness you've let yourself feel. For example, a woman whose husband was sick with cancer was driving past a cemetery with him one day. Suddenly she felt panic in her heart. She wondered why because although she was worried about her husband and loved him dearly, she wasn't panicky about his situation at the time. It came to her that she was feeling his panic in her own body. With that awareness, she could release her feeling of panic and then try to help him with the panic he was feeling. When Carin held the dragonfly and then let it go, she had to think, "If it works, it works. If it doesn't, let it go."

It's not so easy for a compassionate person to let go of the feelings of others, and it's always a temptation to feed one's ego. "Oh I'm so sensitive and caring that I feel the suffering of the world or of John or of Mary, and I will stay with it until it's cured." One has to feel, use the feelings of others to try to help, and then release what isn't one's own.

Darkness

One of my clients, one who uses seeing to access her power, was a woman whose power is very dark. In this chapter, I want to discuss this kind of dark power, its strength, its dangers and burdens, and its potential to help one discern and use one's gifts.

Deirdre came to see me referred by one of my patients who has known her for many years, starting back in Ireland, where they were both born. Deirdre came to this country when she was sixteen with her parents and two siblings. She is the youngest.

She is a tall, strong looking woman with dark red hair, blue Irish eyes, and very white skin. She seemed self-assured and confident as she walked in, shook hands with me, looked me in the eye, and sat down on the couch across from me. Her look was very challenging as though she was looking for a fight. Her actions, however, were more subdued as she crossed her legs, sank back onto the couch, and played with her bottle of water.

Her main complaints were that she was experiencing headaches, was anxious all the time, and had episodes of being very angry. Her initial appearance seemed very different from what I was seeing and feeling around her. On the outside she was reserved but spoke directly and shared with me very well when asked a direct question. I did, however, sense that she did not trust me as a male authority figure at all. On another level, I saw that there was a lot of darkness around her. It made her self-possession and good looks seem faded.

It gave her a feeling of heaviness and gravity. I could see the darkness going back away from her like a stream or river flowing all the way back as far as I could see.

What is this darkness? It is powerful dark energy, energy which was created by her karma. *Karma* is a word much bandied about. People often misuse it to explain or justify themselves. "Oh, I couldn't help marrying the wrong person." "It's my karma to steal; I couldn't help myself." "I'm destined to be lonely/popular, rich/poor, successful/a failure." But karma is not just fate or fatalistic.

Rather, in the Buddhist sense, one's karma is the consequence of past lives. There's a rational cause and effect. It's not just a doom; it's something to recognize, accept, and learn from. One way of putting it is that we have the karma we do in order to learn what we need to learn. If we can see and understand our karma, we can see more clearly who we are, learn to avoid the mistakes of past lives, and create better ways to be. Such learning can be arduous; this isn't just a matter of positive thinking.

To me, there are two kinds of karma. There is your personal karma, life after life, what you've done and what others have done to you. And there's family or ancestral karma.

Take personal karma first. In past lifetimes, Deirdre was used by men, as a slave and as a prostitute. In this lifetime she has problems with men. They have power over her, through money, position, and physical strength. She is attracted to such men and attracts them because she is familiar with this pattern from the past. She has been married two times, both in abusive, violent relationships. Nonetheless, she isn't just a victim though she understandably feels completely like one. When she is angry, she creates violence around her, rouses violence in her partners, and thus helps create the familiar pattern.

Deirdre's ancestral karma is similarly dark. Ancestral karma is the karma of your family, your ancestors, played out in this life time. Each ancestor has his or her own individual karma, of course, but as a group they also convey a weight, a collective karma, as it were. In Deirdre's case, there is darkness all the way back to the famines, the burnings, killings, rapes, and the colonial oppression. So she is playing out both personal and ancestral karma, both of them in this case dark and heavy.

People feel the weight of such darkness. For example, a patient with a middle-European background has a dark cast to her, is prone to depression, has trouble staying in relationships and keeping a job. In my own past lives I abused my power: as a Warrior I killed, and in relationships I attracted and was attracted to women who also had dark power. People with dark karma tend to attract each other, and when they do, they reinforce each other's darkness. They enjoy flirting and feinting with each other; they enjoy teaming up to use their dark power together. Such a relationship is like playing with one's shadow. It's addictive, and when it gets to be too much, the people will repeat what happened in other lifetimes, including pain, power struggles, and even murder.

So what people with dark power need to do first is to recognize what is happening. Before going on to the way Deirdre started to see her power, however, we need to look further at what the dark energy is, how it works. The power is the dark energy; the dark energy is power. It is like electrical current in the wall which you can plug into and use. Or to use another analogy, it is like a powerful dark stream. The movement of the stream is energy, it provides power.

The key is to recognize what it is and to learn how to use it. If you're in the dark stream, if you slip, fall back into it, let it overwhelm you, it will replicate where it came from, what was done to you, what you did in the past. But you don't have to be overwhelmed by the dark energy; you don't have to just repeat the pattern. You can be like a rock in the stream, or you can stand on the bank of the dark river and see your karma and your power. Or, to shift the image, you can be a filter and shape how the energy comes through you. You can channel the electrical current.

Dark power is neither good nor bad in itself. Your energy is what it is; it's what you're born with, what you have to work with. What is important is to concentrate. A person with dark energy can't just say, "Be positive" or "Put out love or affirmative intention" or "Use the law of attraction." Such methods may work for people who are ready and who don't have the dark undertow. But someone like Deirdre needs to concentrate in order to learn what she needs to. Through such concentration, she can channel her power to help her use her gifts. For example, I had to spend years learning to channel the power of dark energy through martial arts to gain the discipline of controlling my behavior. And I've worked hard to channel my power through my heart, through a place of feeling, to use what I see in a way that helps people heal. First, I see in a cold, dark way; then I put what I see in my heart; then I use my power to help.

Deirdre began a similar journey. After we had talked for a while and she had begun to trust me a little, she told me that she had dreams predicting the future, that she could see dead people, that she could see spirits who talked with her whether she wanted them to or not. Even as a child, she had gotten As in school although she never read a book because she could look at the blackboard and see what answers the teacher wanted. She was scared by these experiences and didn't understand what they meant.

As we worked together, she started to learn how to interpret and use such experiences. For example, one night when she was in her late twenties, she started to have nightmares and to feel as if she couldn't move her arms and legs, as if she had no voice and couldn't call out. Such an experience is common to the nightmares many of us have. But Deirdre would then wake up and see a strong man of Asian ancestry standing beside her bed and staring down at her.

She said to me, "I was terrified to be alone in my house, clearly a sign I needed help, so I called you."

So I said, "Why don't you just ask him who he is and what he wants and why he is there?"

"Right. A ghost has been sneaking up on me at night and all I have to do is have a conversation with him? I am much too scared to do so!"

But she heard me when I said that she had the gift of seeing, and she had come to trust me a little. Besides she was pretty desperate. After a few more terrified nights, she asked the ghost, "Who are you?"

The ghost replied, "I am Wong."

That was enough for that night. The next night he came back again. Deirdre repeated her question and got the same answer. She did this for a few more nights and then came back to see me.

"All he keeps saying is that his name is Wong," Deirdre said to me.

"Isn't something else supposed to happen?"

I laughed at this. "You only asked him his name. So he only gave you his name. If you ask other questions, maybe he will answer them."

I went on to explain that souls who come to you in this way usually want or need something from you. That is why they have come in the first place.

Over the next few times she saw Wong, Deirdre was able to piece together the story.

"He told me he was my master in a previous life. He was very abusive. He beat me and raped me many times. Finally, he got tired of me and threw me out onto the street, where I died a little while later." She was clearly very upset by all the memories of this past life.

"He asked what he could do to make amends. He said he needed peace and would do anything I asked of him if only I would forgive him."

At this point Deirdre had a choice to make. She could go the dark power way and use Wong for dark power to help her manipulate others, or she could forgive him and let him go to the light. She was at a crossroads. Which way to go. The path she chose would color the rest of her life and either add to or release some of her karma. That is, if she chose the dark way, it would add more to the dark part of her karma. If she chose to forgive him, she and he would be freed from the patterns of the past and that part of her karma would be released. I told her to go home and think about it.

Since we were in this for healing, I hoped she would choose the Way of Forgiveness. This was the only way she would be able to move her life forward.

The next time I saw her she said, "I think the reason I saw him again was as a test. Do I want to repeat the same patterns as in the past? Or do I want to move on. It is the only reason I can think of that I'm seeing this frightening man and all he's done to me. We are here for healing, right? So I want to forgive him and let him go. How do I do this?"

"What do you feel towards him at this moment?" I asked.

"At first I felt the pain of the past very strongly. Then I was very rageful and now I feel nothing," she said.

I replied, "Then all you have to do is forgive him."

At that moment the power began to build in the room. The air became heavier, there was a buzzing sound, and my physical vision became blurred. I knew this was the feeling when my power showed up. I could actually see Wong and Deirdre as she was when she was with him in their past life together.

Deirdre said out loud, "I forgive you. You are free to go." At that point Wong began moving away toward a tunnel of light and was gone. The room returned to normal.

I congratulated her.

Deirdre laughed and said, "What would you have done if I'd said I wanted to use the Dark Power to hurt him? Would you have helped me then?"

Destroyer

The Destroyer is known to us all. We usually hear about Destroyers as religious leaders, CEOs of major organizations, athletic coaches, and politicians who have power and who can use it to influence others easily. They may also be charismatic people on a smaller scale, such as a therapist who has flocks of devoted people who don't want to leave therapy or a teacher who draws students to become personally attached to him or her. Although we have typically heard more about men as Destroyers, Destroyers may also be women, and we are beginning to hear more about women of this type.

Such people can be gifted leaders or healers. However, unlike other compelling leaders or healers, Destroyers will use their energy to gain power over others, not to help others empower themselves. Think of the difference between Gandhi and Jim Jones.

When I look at a Destroyer, he will seem to be dark, to have a dark smudge over his aura. As noted in the chapter on dark power, dark energy needn't be used harmfully; it can be used for good or for ill. Deirdre's dark energy, for example, comes from her karma and she can learn to use it to help others. I try to use dark power to protect people from those who harm or attack them. And someone with dark energy can become a great teacher or can build a company to create helpful products or jobs.

Such a person, however, may come to want power over others. He will become a Destroyer when he attracts dark power in this life in order to control, manipulate, or draw energy from others. This dark energy will build and build until it ultimately destroys him and those around him.

I met Kieran one day in my office. He was of average height and build with dark brown hair, a very normal-looking person—except for his intensity. He had sharp, light blue eyes which seemed to suck you in when he looked at you. His energy would come right at you and bring you to focus on him. I felt that he could draw attention, curiosity, devotion, even desire. Trained to do psychotherapy and energy healing, Kieran had a successful practice and considerable reputation in the Boston area.

After we'd spent a few minutes getting started, he said, "I'm here to see you because I've been accused of assaulting a patient of mine. I'm shocked that this woman could accuse me of such a thing. But my lawyer thought it might help my defense if I checked in with another therapist so I could get further support for my case that I'm not dangerous." He shook his head and gave a small smile, inviting me to see how ridiculous such a charge was. He lowered his eyes, as if to veil them, and added that he knew he was attractive to women and therefore was very careful to maintain appropriate boundaries.

This situation did not come walking through my door every day, so I took another, closer look at him. The first thing I could see was that the aura around his head looked dark and had a black tinge to it. I recognized this as the beginning of the destroyer power. Increasingly intrigued and careful, I looked even more closely at him; then I could see the basis for this pattern going back to his youth.

People with this pattern usually do not begin by using their ability destructively. The potential is there, however, because even when they are quite young, they may realize that they can read others and can use what they see to influence them. Their charm will get them out of a difficult situation or enable them to talk their way out of trouble.

Kieran told me of a time when he was about ten and he stole some candy from a store. The clerk caught him and brought him to the manager. Instead of denying what he'd done, Kieran looked up at the burly manager out of his clear blue eyes, confessed, and begged him not to tell his mother, for she might beat him if she was in one of her drunken states. In fact, it was true that his mother was an alcoholic. He promised to do whatever the manager wanted by way of punishment. He'd read the man accurately and was let off with a stern warning not to steal again. The best part, however, was that the manager ended up feeling that he'd done a good deed for a promising youngster. Kieran at this age may or may not have been consciously or calculatingly manipulative, but through such experiences, he came to realize that others would follow his lead.

Because he knew about pain from his difficult upbringing, Kieran stayed away from drugs and alcohol himself and wanted to learn how to help others heal from the wounds of their pasts. Given this motivation and given his insight into people and his ability to influence them, it made sense that he studied psychology in school and became a therapist.

While working as a therapist, he was also introduced to a South American shaman who taught him about power and energy. At first he used shamanism to gain insight into his patients' energetic strengths and weaknesses and to help them bring up their own energy as they needed. He worked particularly well with shy people since he could see their issues when they weren't able to say what they needed. People would come to grateful tears at being known at such deep levels. Soon, however, he began to cross appropriate boundaries.

It is true that boundaries are a particularly difficult area for a healer to address. First of all, people who come to a healer are vulnerable because they are hurting and because they want you to reach out to them and help them. Second, you do your best to connect to them in order to see their problem and to help them. This connection can be exciting for a client who senses the energy and understanding.

Over time, such people may come to rely on you, perhaps even becoming emotionally attached to you. They will sense your power and want you to use it to be what they want or to give them what they need. It's tempting for a shaman, or any therapist for that matter, to give clients what they need rather than having them work through what they need themselves. If this happens, they will become dependent on the healer, need him to answer all the questions. So from the beginning I try to maintain boundaries between us so this problem will not get in the way of their healing.

My teacher always warned me about this danger because although she had begun to train many people, only a few ever finished the training because most—both men and women—abused their power. I find I have to question myself continually so as not to fall into this trap.

I need to ask, "Is my compassion for this person genuinely for her or am I mostly wanting to make myself feel good? Am I letting myself slip into too much attraction to her?"

"Am I put off by another person because I'm jealous of or wanting to compete with his abilities?"

"Is another person becoming too dependent on me because I like that he is offering me some of his energy and that he will do what I tell him rather than come to see for himself what he needs?"

"Do I have so much power over this person or this group that no one will confront me? I need to see what is really going on."

"Am I following the guidance of the Universe or of my own self-interested impulses?"

To keep such clarity, I have to remind myself that I am not doing the healing, that I am merely a vehicle for the energy of the universe.

Remembering this makes me mindful that I need to stop and attend to what the Universe suggests the other person needs. When I see what the other person needs or what the other person is wrestling with, I can't just spring into action or act like a Warrior dominating her. I need to take that seeing and put it into my heart, to come from loving that person, not from feeding my own needs or ego.

Kieran fell into the trap of thinking he was doing the healing. Destroyers tend to be seers, and you may remember that one problem seers can have is to become cold and arrogant. Kieran stopped being humble and thus stopped feeling for his patients, losing the ability to stay in his heart. As a result, he started taking his patients' energy for himself.

Here's an example on a larger scale: a powerful teacher started amassing money, power, and women. In his mind, having sex with these women was helping them because he was a vehicle of the divine; he deluded himself into thinking that by having sex with them, he was helping them connect with the divine. This gifted healer lost his way so that his center became the locus of a cult. Or consider a woman I know who had five or six men going at the same time, all totally dependent on her. Or a body-worker who was having sex with one of his clients because "she wanted it" and offered it to him saying it was part of her healing process.

So my task was to try to get Kieran to be balanced, both to see his problem and to work from his heart in dealing with it. This was not going to be easy.

A Destroyer has the ability to see what people need. Furthermore, when you stand in a position of power, it's even easier to see because people tell you what they want; it's blatant. And once Destroyers get such power, they come to depend on it, it's like an addiction. It's like a rock musician who gets a rush from the energy the audience sends, wild with the music and stage performance. The performer can control the energy and gets intoxicated with the power to manipulate the crowd.

Intellectually, Kieran could understand what I was talking about, and he would discuss the theory intelligently, but he never let himself really feel that he was using the power that others gave him for his own benefit, to increase his own power. He evaded the sexual misconduct charge on a technicality (I suspect he figured out how to manipulate the lawyers and the judge), and for a while he behaved himself. I knew that he wasn't going to be able to stop building his power when I had a vision of him in the form of a hawk sweeping down to steal the third chakra energy from one of his patients.

The energy he brought with him became darker and darker, and I had to spend increasing time clearing my office of his energy after his visits. There were no checks on his power, and he continued to feel that he was doing good for others. After about a year, he stopped seeing me, perhaps because he knew he couldn't fool me and didn't get from me the confirmation he wanted. I heard from others that he moved out of state.

Shamanic healing is all about change. Not everyone wants to or can change, and it's particularly hard for Destroyers to be willing to change deeply.

I'm familiar with the lure of dark power over others because of my own past life experiences. I have had visions of at least two past lives in which I've had and abused great power. Once in Spain I was a Warrior with a natural presence, leadership, and physical gifts. Though I was a great soldier, I was not noble born and stepped on the toes of nobles as I tried to make my way to political power. Ultimately I was assassinated. I could also use sexual energy to attract, enjoy, and manipulate women. Now, this time around, in this life, I'm not going to use the dark power for my own benefit. I sense it's there and am attracted to it, but I concentrate in order to be aware of it, recognize it, and not misuse it.

It would be so easy to go there, but I'm not going to do it.

Aphrodite

There are some women who have a fundamental, deep-rooted energy that attracts men and that makes them need men. As with others, the Universal energy coming to the individual is neutral; in the case of the "Aphrodite," this energy is shaped so that her process revolves around men.

Aphrodites may or may not be physically beautiful, they may be young or old; what comes through is an energy that just seems to gather men around them. You may have seen such a woman—she's the one that men move toward at a party or that men feel they can talk to easily, with a little frisson of excitement. Women tend to be jealous of her and can't figure out exactly what it is that makes her so successful with men. She has enormous power.

This power can be expressed in very creative ways. For descriptions of what Jean Shinoda Bolen calls "the alchemical power" of Aphrodite, I recommend her book Goddesses in Every Woman. In this chapter, I'm going to focus on the patterns of Aphrodite power that I see most often in my practice. The women who come to my office tend to have had some difficulty living with their power—and it is a difficult gift—though their potential is amazing.

Even as little girls, Aphrodites seem to attract the notice and attentions of boys and men. Because of this energy, Aphrodites are particularly vulnerable; as little girls, they don't really understand what is happening and therefore can't protect themselves. Furthermore, when they do get old enough to try to protect themselves, their attempts may take forms that hurt them. And finally, because their basic energy is in connection with others, they don't or can't take the path of withdrawal to give themselves respite. Let's look at these issues one step at a time.

As a girl, an Aphrodite may attract the attention and even molestations of the neighborhood boys. Even if she is modest or innocent, she is the one that boys will whistle at, tell stories about, call loose or cheap. Even the men in her own family may respond in hurtful ways. The worst form, of course, is actual abuse, but a father, sensing his daughter's attractiveness, may get angry at her, say that she's dressing provocatively and going to get into trouble. One Aphrodite, for example, was going to a dance with her sisters and cousins. Of the group, she had the most concealing and least provocative dress on, but her father ignored the others and told her she had to change because she was dressing like a slut.

Obviously, such experiences can hurt a girl and cause her to be afraid. She tries to find ways to protect herself. Unfortunately, since she doesn't want to keep attracting attention as she has in the past with such painful results, she may use her Aphrodite energy in ways that twist back on herself, cause her harm.

Let's consider first a couple of patterns of Aphrodites who see, who are seers.

The first way they may try to protect themselves is to put up a wall. This wall feels cold, like transparent steel. In the case where they decide not to let a man get anywhere at all, there's a two part process. (1) First they think about whether to let a man see them.

If they decide not to let a man even see them, he'll just walk by. They will be an ice queen, won't even chitchat, and will act very cold and distant. For example, in a bar a man might start to walk toward such a woman but she'll put up the wall and he'll just keep going, or if he does stop, she'll just freeze him out.

(2) The other early question for seeing Aphrodites is whether or not to let themselves see a man. To do so would mean letting the wall down and opening their heart. If they're fully protecting themselves, they won't let the wall down at all and thus won't let themselves even see the man. This takes some resistance because these Aphrodites, remember, are seers. Even if the Aphrodite lets herself look at the man, she may protect herself by saying she could see in ten seconds that he's not the one for her. She might say, "I looked at all the men and none are good enough." Because she's a seer she'll see everything negative about him, and she may be right, but she won't see the good. Or she might say that no man is good enough for her if he can't figure out how to get through the wall that she's put up precisely not to let any man through. Though she might want to be with a man, she is afraid because of her past experiences and uses her seeing to protect herself.

Another kind of seeing Aphrodite protects herself from the hurt she fears men may cause by becoming manipulative. This Aphrodite uses her ability to see as a way of keeping men at a distance, keeping them from getting too close. When she sees something she wants in a man, she can see into him and figure out how to have him give it to her. Does he need praise? A sense of the chase? Excitement? She may want protection or money or sex or power over him or, through him, power over others. One Aphrodite, for example, wanted to get out of an unhappy marriage, so she attracted another man who would not only have an affair with her but would also marry her after she had divorced her first husband. The woman who is the power behind the throne is so well known as to be a cliché.

Such fear based relationships often run into trouble, however. Such a woman may, for example, feel sexually attracted to a man, and as an Aphrodite, she has no trouble attracting him. But since she is afraid to let him get really close, to completely open her heart with him, she keeps him at enough of a distance that he cannot hurt her. If she feels he's getting too close, she may act so as to send him away. Or she may eventually get bored or tired (manipulating someone else does take energy), and when she does, she will discard him. The loving wife who appreciated her husband's support may decide he's too submissive; the seductive woman who reveled in her lover's energy may find him too demanding. She will use the vulnerabilities she sees in him; perhaps she flirts openly with other men, perhaps she lets him know she doesn't really need him, and without his really understanding what has happened, he's gone and she's attracted another man.

I want to emphasize that for this kind of Aphrodite, as for others, the root issue isn't meanness or evil, it's fear. In spite of her power, she fears what loving might open her to, she may fear leaving a home or a city that feels safe to her, she may fear the sadness of losing what she in fact most wants. And she may be unaware of what she's doing, thinking rather that others are attacking her or letting her down.

Now let's look at the Aphrodite who is a feeler. Such Aphrodites may get abused from a young age because they are open, loving, interested in men, and don't know what they are doing. As feelers, they absorb the energy that others send them, so they may believe they are as others feel about them: trashy, stupid, no-good.

Having a man is a necessity for her, as for other Aphrodites, and the key for her is to feel safe. As a feeler, however, she can't protect herself by acting cold. One way she might maintain a sense of control is to attract a man who is emotionally needy or emotionally limited. Such a man is easy to attract, thus giving her a sense of power. Also, as a feeler she knows how to act loving toward him whatever happens, and thus feels needed. Or she may feel attracted to the little boy in him and not be able to see the rest; she's attracted to the part of him that isn't hurtful.

The sad irony is that such men often abuse their women, may keep them in the house, cheat on them, and dictate everything they can do. Psychologically, one can say that the woman is repeating a pattern she learned early in her life. On an energetic level, she is trying to do whatever she can to stay heart connected to her man. Why doesn't she leave? There may be one piece of the man she fell in love with. For example, although he may lose his job, drink, or expect her to deal with the mess he makes, he may be able to intervene when her family tries to attack her. If the man is controlling, she may think that if she does everything he dictates, she will be safe, and she's good at sensing what he wants. Think of Marilyn Monroe as an archetype of someone who is so compelling and yet so vulnerable. She married men who could give her what she felt she lacked, like intellectual accomplishment from Arthur Miller.

Another way for a feeling Aphrodite to try to protect herself is to make herself feel ugly. She may gain or lose too much weight, she may wear baggy clothing, or she may deliberately go against whatever is considered fashionable. When she tries to hide who she really is, however, she may actually become sick; all that power is submerged and directed against herself.

Sometimes the young Aphrodite starts to feel anger, then rage, at how she is treated. The rage can get darker and lead to manipulation. Feeling Aphrodites tend to manipulate in a passive-aggressive way, through guilt, drama, and whining. Or the feeling

Aphrodites may turn their rage against themselves for attracting the kind of attention they do. When they attack themselves, they can fall into drinking, drugs, or self-mutilation (consider the rise in cutting among adolescents). The hardest turn this self-rage can take is toward illness. Such an Aphrodite may have a series of illnesses, one thing after another, ranging in severity from headaches to cancer.

Our contemporary culture is toxic for Aphrodites. The highly sexualized movies, television shows, ads, and images in magazines. The ways that models dress (or undress) in popular magazines. The fads among students such as bare midriff tops and low-slung tight pants. Given such sexualization, Aphrodites can't hide behind the floor-length full skirts of old; and traditional coming-of-age rituals often take on a modern gloss of young teens dressing and acting like sexy women. Nowadays, it's considered a compliment for a teenage girl to be called "hot," and many girls pose for provocative pictures on Myspace thinking it's all just fun. Such a culture is demanding of all young women and the young men who respond to them, but it particularly channels the Aphrodite energy and desire for men into highly sexualized forms. The dangers here are obvious. Moreover, if society places a high value on sex appeal, Aphrodites are the queens, and this is going to make other women jealous of them.

So where are hurt Aphrodites going to go? Maybe either the cold wall or the abusive relationship. They don't have the option of just staying away from men for a while because being connected is central for them; Aphrodites can't gain respite through withdrawing. Even maintaining the cold wall takes energy, and at a basic level, they are still looking for connection.

Here's another way that Aphrodite energy can be difficult: an Aphrodite will always attract men, and her current man may come to resent this. What man wants to fall in love with a woman he can't have for himself? And it's pretty hard for a man to pay attention to a woman and court her all the time. When he can't, she may get bored and go find someone she thinks will. Feeling Aphrodites may get sick or resentful at how they are treated and yet act in ways they think will keep pleasing their men.

However, when such a woman starts to realize that something's amiss, that she's hurting, that somehow her power is blocked, she can start to change. She may first seek help from a physician or a therapist. But when the problems seem intractable by ordinary means, she may end up in my office.

One patient, for example, had been treated by a series of physicians. There was real illness, but each time the doctors did something to treat a problem, another would arise. Surgery helped her endometriosis, but then her back started to cause such pain that she had more surgery. Still hindered by back pain, she also developed an autoimmune disorder. Feeling hopeless and exhausted, when a friend told her about my work, she figured that she had nothing to lose. When she arrived, she acted like the model patient. On a subtler level, like other Aphrodites, she was trying to attract me, and she was very attractive. Dressed in a tight black leather jacket and long skirt, she would cross her legs demurely, but her tasseled boots caught the eye each time she moved. That compelling energy was there underneath all the pain and politeness.

When I see that a woman is an Aphrodite, I know she's trying to do what comes naturally to her, trying to attract me. I let these women know that I see what the dynamic is, I set clear and firm boundaries, and I offer assurance that I won't hurt them but will protect them. Their next realization is that if there's a man who can see through the wall and not be destructive within the safety of my office, they can be and explore who they are. But it's a long process because it's so natural for them to act as they do, because they've often suffered such hurt, and because they're so used to protecting themselves. Often there's also denial since the patterns started very young, before they realized what they were doing and what was being done to them.

The most important step for an Aphrodite is to realize that she's always going to attract men and need men, that's just who she is—she hasn't done anything wrong, and neither have they. Once she can accept this, she can channel her Aphrodite energy in constructive ways and avoid some of the dangers to herself and others. What she needs in any situation is awareness of how she's acting and reacting and of how others are responding to her.

A seeing Aphrodite may be able to catch what's going on and see ways to use her gift positively. A woman who knows and enjoys the responses of men to her, instead of entangling them, can sprinkle a bit of her magic on them, like pixie dust, and then move on and let them move on, leaving pleasure but no harm done. She doesn't get angry at how the men react to her and knows she hasn't been an evil temptress. Or she may channel her gift into becoming a charismatic teacher who charms her students but also knows appropriate limits. As a manager, she may see what is necessary and figure out how to motivate the men on her staff. As a healer, she may know how to help a person struggling with chronic illness by using his desire to please her to keep him taking his medicines.

A feeling Aphrodite can also transmute her energy to positive forms. If she decides she wants to take care of herself, she can use her energy to attract people who can help her. She can make doctors want to work with her even if her condition is frustrating, and she can choose helpers who genuinely want what's best for her rather than those who want to use her. She can also attract people who would benefit from her working on them. In this way she can act like a Loving Healer. She may not be able to go so far as someone whose greatest gift is healing through love, but she can bring love to children, animals, and those in need. Some Aphrodite mothers are mercurial, charming their children when present but also likely to take off and leave them for periods of time. But others are devoted mothers, like one I know who not only is a loving, creative, and patient mother to her son, who has cerebral palsy, but also has become a resource for other parents, who turn to her for encouragement and practical suggestions.

Both kinds of Aphrodites have become successful actors. Their quality just exudes off the screen or stage. It's alluring—what every woman wants to be and what every man wants. They stir up high drama, love it, and love being the center of attention. Not many movies are made about women who are quiet, supportive keepers of the domestic flame. When you look at a scene in a movie or on television, notice which woman your eye keeps going to. Someone once said that Judy Garland was the only person who could dance with Fred Astaire and keep drawing your eye to her rather than letting you focus on him. Creative Aphrodites tend to be noticed for themselves as well as for their work. We know about Frida Kahlo, not just about her paintings.

Most women have some Aphrodite traits. In fact most of us have more than one pattern. The women in whom Aphrodite dominates have both unusual challenges and unusual power. They light up a room; with awareness, they can use that light to benefit both themselves and others.

Hyperfocus

People who have the gift of hyperfocusing may be men or women, but they are always seers. Seeing doesn't necessarily mean that they have optical images, though they may; rather, it means that they see from the third eye, which in the chakra system is located between and a little above the physical eyes. The energy from the third eye gives one insight.

This insight in hyperfocus people may take the form of visions, or a quick grasp of the steps of a process, or the solution to a musical problem, or a swift movement with a sword. In all cases, however, what calls up the special concentration is having something to focus on—it could be a problem, a project, a person, calling a soul, or anything. An artist, for example, may be working on a painting and focus so intently that everything else in the room disappears.

Here's what happens when a person hyperfocuses: I feel the energy in the room increasing in a tight beam coming from his third eye. I can feel it, sense it, see it, tap into it. It's as if a switch is turned on, and I can feel the energy as an intensity or a pressure; I may even jerk my head back as I tap into it or as it hits me. This energy is hard to describe, but think of a beam or a tunnel of energy that vibrates at a very high rate. It doesn't have a color, it can be light though it's usually darker, and it is clear. The tighter the person's focus, the tighter the beam or tunnel and the more intense the vibration of the energy.

Let me give you an example. I know a man who is a master of medieval sword technique and history. When I challenge him, come at him either with the sword or with a problem about the sword, he hyperfocuses on the steps of the problem. Then he comes back at me powerfully and very quickly with the sword move or with the solution.

Now, what is going on when the person does this? The person will see all kinds of possibilities, then by hyperfocusing will jump into a clear space. This jump is when the person is connecting with the Universal energy. It doesn't matter whether she is focusing on the steps of a process, a feeling or experience, or an intellectual puzzle. At a certain point, the thinking, tussling, and puzzling will drop away and the Universal energy will flow through her and she will be wholly focused, will be in the clear space, will let her third eye (or the unconscious if you will) take over from the thinking mind.

This process is what Zen uses koans for. A koan has no logical answer; it's impossible to solve by ordinary means. How do you know the sound of one hand clapping or what your face was before you were born? By focusing your mind on a logically impossible question, the koan gets you to the point where the mind lets go and you just let the energy move you. A scientist can use an intellectual problem the same way. Isaac Asimov, for example, wrote that he would tussle with a problem and then go to a movie to let his unconscious mind continue working on the problem; when he did so, the solution sometimes floated up. What he was doing was using the problem as a koan and the movie as a way to relax his conscious mind, to let him get to a different place, to where the third eye could take over.

The goal, as explained in *Zen and the Art of Archery,* is to get to that clear place where you don't aim and shoot the arrow, but the target draws the arrow. Such an experience happened to Padraig. He was an outdoor, survival kind of person and recently took a class on making a bow the way Native Americans or medieval bowmen used to make them. Unlike modern bows, which have pulleys, sights, and gadgets to make aiming and pulling the string easier, the bow Padraig was working on was to have just wood and gut string. Here's how he described what happened:

"As usual the work sucked me in. I was very intrigued by it, the choice of tree, the way the grain of the wood is used, the techniques for shaping the wood. After a week of working on my bow, other ideas kept coming into my head—maybe I didn't have the best wood; maybe I should try two or three different kinds of trees; maybe I wasn't shaping my wood right. I would get an idea and then think, no that's not the best way, let me try something else, how about this or that. It was very difficult; I could feel the other ideas pulling at me, pulling at me. They would wake me up at night and disturb my work during the day. They really were like demons."

I suggested to Padraig that whenever a distracting idea or dissatisfaction came into his mind, whenever a demon pulled at him, he should write it down.

He agreed to try.

"Whenever a distracting idea or piece of information tugged at my mind, I wrote it down and got back to my work. Finally I finished the bow. Then I bought some arrows because I wanted to shoot the bow right away. Out in the woods, I set up a target about seventy-five feet away, one of those practice targets with the black bull's eye in the middle. I began to shoot.

"The bow had a very heavy pull, maybe a sixty pound pull, and I had not shot a bow in a number of years. Besides, even the bows I had shot were compound bows, not like this basic one, so it took a while before I could hit the target, and when I did finally hit the target, I never got the bull's eye.

"As I concentrated on the bull's eye, I began to feel a power come over me. I was focusing very intently. A tunnel opened in front of me connecting me to the target. It seemed like the target was pulling the arrow to it. The arrow went to the bull's eye. I picked up another arrow and the same thing happened. I got so excited that I lost my focus and the next arrow missed the target completely. I worked at getting back to that place. I realized that when I focused and the tunnel opened up, nothing mattered, not the draw of the bow or anything else. We were all just one. By concentrating and focusing clearly, I went to a place I had never been."

Once Padraig got to that clear space, he and the target became one; he was in the tunnel and the tunnel pulled the arrow. When this happened, when he kept this focus, the arrow found the bull's eye. When he lost the hyperfocus and tried to aim in the normal way, tried to control the flight of the arrow, he missed.

Padraig's story demonstrates how hyperfocusing works. It also shows how it can be blocked. One obstacle for hyperfocusing people is the quickness with which their minds jump to alternatives and multiple possibilities. Because they're so quick, when they encounter a challenge, they may see all kinds of options and problems. This plethora of ideas can be helpful, like brainstorming, but it can also block their power. There may be too much information coming in, so they get distracted. Or, unable to choose, they may get frozen and be unable to go anywhere.

Another obstacle is suggested by Padraig's use of the word "demons." When he called the ideas that distracted him "demons," he was echoing a term Buddhists sometimes use to characterize temptations or destructive emotions or, most broadly, delusions. A delusion is an idea or feeling in our mind that we mistakenly think is real. For example, we may think a person is the one to make us happy, so we may project onto him or her the traits we think desirable; but the traits are our wishes, not necessarily the real traits of the other person, so we delude ourselves. The idea was just in our head, not in the real other person.

Similarly, a feeling or emotion is just a feeling or emotion; our being depressed doesn't mean the world is making us miserable. To be sure, the world may be brutal, but getting depressed is how we are responding to the world. It's not wrong to see pain in the world or to feel it ourselves, but we need to be aware that this is our vision and our feeling about the situation. We have ideas and feelings, of course, and these are ways we structure our world. What is crucial is that we need to know these are OUR feelings and beliefs and to try to keep them from causing ourselves or others harm.

Padraig's delusion was that he had to or could make the perfect bow. His mind kept chasing after alternatives, hoping that each would get him to perfection. He thought the wood was too thin or the notch for the bowstring was too deep or he should start all over again, and again and again, making this or that adjustment. Of course, sometimes we do think of ways to improve something we're working on, and sometimes it's helpful to experiment, to mess up, and to learn from mistakes. But this constructive process is different from what was hindering Padraig. What he needed to see was that he was beset by the demon of perfection. There's no such thing as perfection, and even if there were, Padraig never would have believed he'd reached it.

Another kind of delusion that can distract someone from hyperfocusing is fear. We all feel fear; fear can help us evade danger, but it can also paralyze us when we'd be better off acting. It's not bad or good in itself. It's just a feeling, and we can decide how to respond to it and whether to act or not act on it. Fear is often a problem for Hyperfocusers who are artists, musicians, or dancers. They may have visions or ideas but cannot seem to complete any of them because of fear.

The deepest fear is the ego's fear of letting go. When one hyperfocuses and takes the leap into the clear space, when one connects with the power of the Universe, it's not the ego that acts, it's the Universal power that does. The ego is used to being the part of ourselves, which deals with the world. In Freud's terms, the ego negotiates with reality; it has the job of protecting and advancing the self in the world, of controlling our impulses, and of keeping us from being crushed by the demands of the superego. The ego, the small self, is what we feel gives us some control in the world and some control of ourselves. It's terrifying to let go of that which lets us feel like a self and just to be a channel for a power that comes through us, a power that is not in fact ours.

Realistically, an artist knows that to attain mastery, he or she must learn techniques, practice, and make adjustments and improvements. This is the correct wisdom of the ego. Still, an artist can practice technique forever, but the greatest music will not come just from technique, the dance will not become magic only because of strong muscles. This is not to say that disciplined practice is not necessary for great art. Of course it is. It just isn't enough. When someone asked Yo Yo Ma whether his facial expressions and bodily movements when he played the cello were partly showmanship, he replied no, rather the musician must bring himself and the listener into the music, must lose himself to create the world of the composer through the music. Michelangelo said that the form emerges from the block of marble.

Fiona was a very pretty redhead, around thirty-five years old. When she came to see me, she was suffering from headaches, anxiety, and insomnia from the intense dreams she would have. I saw that she was totally disconnected from the Universe and from her power, from using the Universe's power in her gift.

I felt the potential strength of her energy, but what I felt was different from the way she actually presented herself. Far from being focused, she was scattered. First she talked about her headaches, then she looked out the window and commented on the increasing warmth of the spring sun, then she started talking about the astronomical equinox, then she was off to observations on the harmony of the spheres. I wanted to yell, "Stop! Don't waste that power!" But I knew that the jumping around was a defense mechanism. As soon as a fearful hyperfocuser feels some power, she has to move on. Being who she is, she has to hyperfocus, but she doesn't want to because of the risk. I had my work cut out for me.

At first we talked about her symptoms. She was quick and intelligent, so she saw right away that they didn't have any immediate cause in her present life. So I asked her what she had most loved doing in the past. I was trying to get at what the power was that she was blocking.

It turned out that she had previously expressed her intense energy through playing the violin. In fact, she'd been a child prodigy, had played with symphony orchestras starting when she was only twelve, and had given many solo performances. The critics especially noted the intensity of her energy, the clarity of her tone, and the smoothness of her musical lines. She had met Isaac Stern when she was fourteen and played with him. Then when she was eighteen, she quit playing.

I asked her what had happened.

"I used to practice three to six hours a day. In the beginning, it was fun. I got lots of attention and I loved to play. It seemed so natural to me. My mother, who was a music teacher, used to sit with me for every moment I practiced. When I was young, this was fine because it was time with her and because I wanted to please her.

"As time went on, though, she got more and more demanding. 'Watch your rhythm,' she would say, counting out the time with the metronome; 'go over that part again, you can do better. You need to practice more.' When I got to be a teenager, I wanted to do other things too. There were boys, and I wanted to spend more time on studying math and on reading. You know how it is, kids don't want to be with their parents all the time any more."

"You got that right," I said.

"I rebelled and would fight her and try not to practice. She would force me to sit there and play, and when 1 wouldn't push myself, she would call me lazy or even slap me. I couldn't wait to go away to college. Once I got there, I never played again."

As is the case with Aphrodites, Fiona's gift was expressed when she was very young, so she was vulnerable to exploitation. At first she was pleased at her mother's attention and approval, but as she got older and the pressure became more intense, she rebelled by refusing to play anymore. But to stop the flow of power that she had channeled into playing, she tried to clamp down on everything. Her fear of what her power had led to was keeping her from connecting to it.

I knew right away that she was a powerful seer and that the only way for her to move forward was to face her fear and reclaim her power.

I told her that her headaches, anxiety, and insomnia came from having blocked her power. She didn't really understand what I was talking about.

"You finally got through to me when you pointed out that I was very good at having visions of what to do, but could never finish anything. I had danced, sung a little bit, and done some painting. I had fooled around with other instruments, but it never came to anything. I was embarrassed because I thought I should have been successful at something.

"You got my defenses down. But then you suggested I take up the violin again. I was terrified. I was right back being a teenager again. I thought you were harsh to suggest going back to what I'd tried to leave behind. Still, you'd seen right through me, and I could see what you were talking about. I was pretty miserable and was getting worse, and no other therapy had helped, so I had to try it your way."

It was difficult for Fiona to begin the process, but I felt she needed to go back to the violin. Other music or art would not allow her the opportunity to face her fear. Of course she didn't feel it as opportunity but as terror. Old unresolved emotions have a way of keeping their charge.

I instructed her to play by just playing, I told her, "Don't try to be the concert violinist you once were. Let it take you on a journey. Do not try to control it the way you were trained to do."

Her first reaction was, "There's only one way to play the violin; how can I just let go?" She started to make all kinds of excuses about why she could not play and could not do what I wanted. "I'm classically trained, I can't just scrape away like some fiddler in a restaurant." "My fingers are stiff and I've lost the pads on my fingers."

She went home and tried but came back the next week and reported that just picking up the violin made her shake. She knew she was afraid, out of practice, unable to change her approach.

"You pointed out to me that these thoughts in my head were not real. They were real thoughts, but they were a projection of my fear trying to keep me from connecting to my power. So I made myself play and concentrated on staying with it. Your combination of pressure and kindness helped a lot. Oh, ok, and I didn't want to look like a total incompetent."

Fiona did persevere and after three more sessions reported that she was beginning to enjoy the actual feel of the playing. She stopped worrying about whether she was as good as she or her mother had thought she should be. A month later, she came into my office carrying her violin. She said that she had a strong feeling that she wanted to play with me there.

Then something wonderful happened. As she described it, "I began to play. You sat there and smiled. Somehow the power in the room began to increase as it sometimes does when you want things to happen. I could feel the vibrations in the room, and the surroundings disappeared. I felt the power flow through my third eye and into my heart and then out the violin. I realized that the violin was playing itself and that I was being drawn forward into something.

"I suddenly had a vision of my mother watching me play. There was an intense feeling of love and I could see light flowing from me and surrounding her. She smiled and then seemed to fade away. It was really quite beautiful. I felt that I had gone through something that allowed me to let go of my fear of the instrument and of my mother.

I felt lighter than I had for years."

Fiona had gotten off her path because of her mother and thus had felt she needed to protect herself (her ego, her small self). What she did when she played again was two-fold. First, she focused on playing in a way that let the power of the Universe come through her as her gift expressed it—through the violin. The hyperfocusing brought her through the barrier between the conscious and the unconscious mind, through what Zen Buddhists call "the gateless gate." Then, once she was there, in that clear space, her heart opened spontaneously. It was beautiful to see the rapture and love in Fiona's eyes.

Needless to say her symptoms disappeared.

One other obstacle, or problem, that Hyperfocusers need to be aware of can arise in their dealings with other people. Hyperfocusing people can get very impatient, particularly with people who are feelers rather than seers. Feeling, as you may recall, is a slower process than seeing. It's just as good, just different. Feelers may get to the same clear space of connecting with the power of the Universe, but their route is more careful. They have to protect themselves against taking on other people's stuff and from getting hurt whereas seers are able to be detached and cold, and thus can risk jumping more quickly.

Though they may get impatient with those slower than themselves, hyperfocusing people love to be together because they can join together in the beam and take off. Think about a time when you've seen people focus on a problem and get excited together, talking over each other as they leap to insights and solutions.

An example of Hyperfocusers helping each other is the way Judy and I sometimes work together on this book. When we're discussing a tangled idea, she may have the insight to ask acute questions, and in doing so helps me get clearer about what I'm thinking. But beyond this more common function of questions, she can also feed me energy from the third eye and I'll ride that energy, like riding the wind, and come up with a deeper understanding and articulation of what I want to say. She's feeding me energy in a way similar to the way the Love Healer fed love to the dragonfly to bring it back to life.

As with all healing and helping, this function of a Hyperfocuser works best only if he does not attach to the process or outcome. A teacher who's a Hyperfocuser may quickly see what a student needs to learn or do, but telling the student what to do won't work. The teacher may want to hurry to the right answer, but the student won't really "get it" until she is ready and can take the steps to understand it in her own way. Furthermore, if the Hyperfocuser wants credit or praise, i.e., to feed the ego, he won't get to that clear place and send the purest energy to help.

Once Hyperfocusers have experienced the intense connection that leads them to the tunnel or the beam, the channeling of the Universe's power, they can practice and learn to get themselves there faster. Just as a runner trains for a marathon, running a little farther, then a little farther, the Hyperfocuser can hone the skill and strengthen the mind. Because I've been training for years, now I can go quickly to hyperfocus without needing to analyze; I just go there. Another hyperfocuser says she can see my eyes shift and she knows I'm instantly connected.

The way to strengthen one's skill is to practice focusing. It doesn't matter what the focus is on. Meditation, with or without koans, is one method of training the mind to focus and to let go of irrelevancies. Or a person can practice by focusing on a mathematical problem, on chanting or praying, on studying scripture, on making music or art or anything else. Working on single-pointed concentration will develop this powerful gift.

In the *Bahagavadgita,* Arjuna says to Krishna,

"The mind is restless, unsteady,
turbulent, wild, stubborn;
truly it seems to me
as hard to master as the wind."

Krishna replies,
   "You are right, Arjuna: the mind
   is restless and hard to master;
   but by constant practice and detachment
   ir can be mastered in the end."

                    (6.35, Mitchell translation)

Warrior

The Warrior is one of the best known and popular of the shamanic patterns. In fact, when people think of shamans, they usually think of a Warrior, someone like Castaneda's Don Juan or a Native American medicine man or the "Peaceful Warrior." Most people want to be a Warrior, just as they may want to be the quarterback in football or the ace hurler in baseball. It's hard to accept the gift that one has. What most don't realize is that it's hard to be a Warrior too.

Because Warriors work with power directly and need to build their power to do their rightful work, they have to learn to use it properly. In fact, the power of the Warrior comes from the energy of the Universe; the power comes when you focus this energy for your own use. You can use it well or badly. It's very easy to misuse Warrior power: Warriors can slip into using their power to manipulate others, to gain control over them, to harm others for their own ends. Think of all the gurus who have used their power to seduce followers, to get rich, or to conquer and subdue others.

Warrior shamans are always trying to gain power. When they go bad, they gain power by stealing other people's energy. Such theft happened to a woman who came to see me. She was usually strong and healthy, but she had started feeling washed out, then she developed a bad cold, which lasted for a month, then her back weakened to the point where she had trouble walking. This incremental weakening began after she had been seeing a certain shaman for healing. During a shamanic drumming session she and I did together, she had a vision in which a raven dropped like a thunderbolt into her abdomen and took residence there. The shaman's totem animal was a raven. We could see that he had come in and stolen her energy. I needed to help her distance herself from him, heal the wound in her aura, and make sure he did not come back. Once this happened, she started to feel better.

The proper use of power is to protect, to heal, to serve, and to act in a selfless way for others. Gandhi spoke of making one's life an offering; the medieval knights at their best had an ideal of serving, and doing so honorably. The idea is not to fight for one's own benefit but to fight to protect others from harm.

There's a story of a great Japanese swordsman who lived in the mid-1800s. He was a big man, 6'2", 240 pounds, huge for that time in Japan. He used his ability and his size to beat up and kill others. When he was in his late twenties, he challenged a master to fight using live swords. He charged at the master, a much smaller man, but couldn't move him. At that moment he realized he needed to learn something. What he needed to learn was to let go of his ego, his own pleasure in fighting, and his thinking that he was the powerful one.

When a Warrior thinks he is the one who's powerful, his ego is attaching to the power and thinks that he's the one who's making all this power, that he's the one who's such a great swordsman. When he feels this way, he can easily misuse the power for his own selfish purposes. In reality, it's the energy of the Universe, which is given to and flows through the Warrior; so instead of being proud, the Warrior needs to be humble. The key to this whole thing is being humble. Of course, when power is involved, it's hard to be humble. Consider exceptional athletes: we dislike the athletes who are arrogant. The ones we respect are the ones who are modest and who treat their abilities as a gift. Think about the difference between Joe Domaggio and Roger Clemens.

A Warrior not only serves, but also has to wait to see how he or she is drawn to serve. When someone comes into my office, I look to see whether there's darkness, something threatening or draining. If I do see darkness or danger, I can't let my ego direct me, saying, "I'm so powerful I can get rid of the darkness" or "Oh I want to make him feel better." I have to pause and see whether I am called to do something about it. Someone who's suffering may say, "Make it go away, you have the power!" But I won't by myself leap into action to make anything go away. I feel around, keep moving and probing, wait to see whether I'm drawn to the energy around the person and whether I'm called to do something about it. I don't mean being called necessarily in a religious sense, more a feeling that something is moving me to go THERE or do THIS. Then when something does happen, it's the greater energy flowing through me, not my own individual power.

Sure I can make things happen, but if I let my ego direct me, I'll get corrupted. To stay pure, a Warrior has to live by a code: honor, loyalty, trust. There are certain lines you don't cross. If you give your word, that's it. If you promise fidelity in marriage, you don't have affairs. If you want to end the marriage, you do that first and then go on. In the *Bahagavadgita,* Krishna teaches the Warrior Arjuna:

> Know what your duty is
> and do it without hesitation.

For a Warrior, there is nothing better
than a battle that duty enjoins....
Indifferent to gain or loss,
to victory or defeat,
prepare yourself for the battle
and do not succumb to sin.

(2.31,2.38, Mitchell translation)

I'll try here to break down the process by which I work. Doing so is difficult because usually what happens is very fast. But when I reflect back, these are the steps I see. First I scan with hyperfocus and look with the third eye. I'm always attracted to darkness or to vibrations, which are not smooth, which don't seem to be what they should be. An analogy would be a policeman who's using a scanner to monitor traffic. He may see all the cars going between sixty-five and seventy, but what catches his attention is the car that's cutting in and out, breaking the pattern. Similarly, any vibration that doesn't feel right will attract my scanner. It will pull me toward it.

Then I'll pause and wait to see whether I'm called to do anything. This pause is crucial because working with dark power is dangerous. If as a Warrior, you're going to fight darkness, you usually have to use some dark power too. You may, for example, be killing for a good reason, but it's still killing. So there has to be awareness. Like a physician who can use digitalis or aconite to heal but can also use it to kill, the Warrior uses dark energy to gain power to fight darkness, but he must be very careful. If I feel excited after using dark power, I know that my ego is attached. No matter what I've accomplished, afterwards I should be just as I was before, not all pumped up.

If I'm called to do something, power starts to build around me. Sometimes, however, I can see something but the power doesn't build. Then I know I'm supposed to leave the situation alone. Perhaps the person has to work out his karma himself or he might need to work at releasing a dark soul which is attached to him. There are also times when people just need to get a little space. For example, 1 may see that a dark soul is sucking life from someone, but not be called to get rid of it. Then I may make a space between the person and the soul so she can look at it and find a way to deal with the issue. I can step in the middle, create space and light. There are also times when the darkness disappears when I just show up.

But if the vibration of power builds around me, I know I'm being drawn to do more. Something may happen instantaneously, or there may be a voice or a vision guiding me. Usually there's just a knowing. I go to the cold, clear place, and the power comes through me. The amount that comes through me is whatever's appropriate for what needs doing. People may then even feel the room moving. Sometimes I'll open a door, like a black hole, and the darkness around the other person is moved through that door to another universe. Other times I have to negotiate with the darkness, not with words exactly, more with communicating the feeling "you need to leave."

When I'm looking at something and the tension builds very strongly, the object I'm looking at and everything else in the scene turns red; then if the energy builds even more, the color turns to blue, and then even to white. It's like the scenes you see in movies where everything is viewed through night vision goggles. This happens like a powerful clap of thunder, a wave of energy. Or think of the huge wooden ram used to ring a bell in a monastery, one which takes ten monks to move. When energy like this gets focused into power and comes at something, either the object gets pushed hard—very hard—or it disintegrates.

There are beings around me that I may use to help me do the work. They may be spirit guides, sacred animals, or souls, but in all instances they are dark. I may call on them, or I may be looking at something and they just appear. I can see them around me and can marshal them, rather like being the director or the general. Animals can sense them around me and tend to take off. Once when I was in a high Colorado meadow, the stillness became unnatural—no bird sounds, no rustle of animals; the birds and animals must have felt the power vibrating and the beings present. There's one seer who could actually see these beings around me and was afraid that if she made me angry, I'd marshal them against her, but I wouldn't do that. I could, but that's not what I'm supposed to do in this lifetime.

If I were attacked or if I felt threatened psychically or physically, however, that would be another matter. A Warrior protects himself or herself, partly because that's just how Warriors react to threats. Also, there's a need for alertness because the way some people react to a Warrior is to challenge him or her. I'm always scanning to see and feel the energies around me. When I go into a restaurant, for example, I always scan the room and seat myself so I can be in a position to sense the energies and to place myself where it feels safest.

There have been times when others have tried to use me, put me down, or control me; what they want is for me to use my power in their service. Someone may try to convince me to give popular seminars to boost his own ego, or someone may try to persuade me to favor her in a group. In such instances, where direct attack is not the issue, I've learned not to lash out and no longer get angry with them or want to wound them. I just don't stay near them or let them stay near me. I want to be around people who are okay with who they are and who let me be who I am.

Warriors are no different from other people in needing to protect themselves. Moreover, all patterns need to build their power,
to keep their auras strong, without cracks or holes, so that when
vibration builds, they are strong enough to hold the energy. For
Warriors this is even more important because they are working
with power directly, not through, for example, hyperfocus or love.

Power works on different levels. It may be physical energy, psy-
chic/ mental energy, or spiritual energy—the whole body-mind
spectrum. Bodily energy is obviously of the physical body, one's
feeling of physical strength and vigor. Mind/psychic energy keeps
emotions on an even keel, helps one keep from attaching to things,
and enables the mind to stay clearly focused. Spiritual energy is
connection to the Universe, which is the deepest elemental energy.

People who are damaged will dissipate or waste their energy.
They will get tired, sick, feel a lack of connection to others and
even to their own bodies and minds. One can think of this as having cracks in one's aura that let the energy leak through, letting
energy drain away from the physical, mental, or spiritual being.
There are various causes of such cracks, but we can work to
strengthen our being.

To avoid dissipating one's physical energy, it's important to get
enough sleep, to keep the body in good physical shape, and to be
moderate and mindful in eating and drinking. For mental and
emotional well-being, it's important to keep the mind sharp and
to avoid the stress that causes emotions to flit around and the
mind to be distracted. The practices here are myriad, from meditating to enjoying each day's contentment.

One can strengthen spiritual energy just by doing the work,
whatever one's work is according to one's gifts; a healer needs to
work on developing his healing skills, and a Warrior needs to work
on living according to the Warrior code and working to free

people from darkness. Fundamental to such gifts, and crucial for developing spiritual energy is connecting to the Universe. Sometimes it helps to go into the woods, retreat to a monastery, and have a quiet time and place in one's own home in order to have a respite from distractions. Buddha withdrew three times a day to meditate; he and his monks withdrew during the rainy season. Religious people withdraw to prayer. Wiccans withdraw to the woods. Whatever will help one stay connected—and the more one stays connected, the more the energy builds.

In order to fight darkness, a true shamanic Warrior consolidates his power by harnessing the dark energy. Following a code of honor and striving not to let the dark power twist her, the Warrior strives to bring the power to the service of light.

The Elemental

The Power Behind the Patterns

The Elemental

The Power Behind the Patterns

As the previous chapters have said, different gifts work best with different problems. Not everyone can help with every difficulty. A person who heals through love wouldn't have been able to free Ian from what possessed him, but a Warrior could. I couldn't have brought the dragonfly back to life, but a Love Healer could. A Hyperfocuser may attract men, but she'll never achieve the ability of an Aphrodite; and while an Aphrodite may intuitively know what a man wants, she'll not achieve the Hyperfocuser's unique ability to cut through and solve a problem.

You may have noticed, however, that in all cases, I've talked about the person stepping into a place where he or she goes beyond his or her individual power and connects to the greater power, what I've called the Universe or the One. Many can heal, but what makes a great Healer is being able to tap into this wider power. Many can become strong fighters, but the great Warrior taps into this wider power too.

Here I'm going to talk about this greater or elemental power. First there is The One. Various religions or belief systems have called it such names as The Tao, God, Goddess, Great Spirit, Yahweh, Brahman, etc. It is sheer energy. My belief is that this

One, this sheer energy, is not good energy or bad energy. It exists simply as energy, it's neutral. We can't really say anything about it because to talk about it makes it an intellectual concept. And as soon as it's a concept, we can think of its opposite too. But this energy has no *opposite or limit. Perhaps that's why the ancient Hebrews would not or could not pronounce the sacred name of God.*

Taoists say after the One, comes the Two. We can think about yin and yang, male and female, good and bad, dark and light. As soon as we think in terms of the Two, we can bring the Universal energy into our world, think about it, and describe it.

Here's how I think about the energy brought into the world:

Think of it as a spectrum. Energy which is light starts as pleasant and warm, the kind of light and warmth one feels going out on a nice spring day and sitting in the mild sunlight. As one gets further from the center, light energy can get harmful, like going into the Australian desert in the summer when temperatures reach 130 degrees and can cause one to burn and die. Light enables us to see, and it can also blind us. Another way to think of this energy is as the archetypal or elemental female energy in the world, as the goddess energy. Note that though we first think of goddesses as nurturing and benevolent, they can also be destructive. Kali or Shakti or Hera can be healing and nurturing, or they can be wild and free and dangerous.

Energy that is dark can also start as pleasant, like a December night when moonlight illuminates the snow, cold and clear, luminous and beautiful. The farther out the spectrum of dark energy one goes, the colder and more condensed it gets. Finally it too can become destructive as the Antarctic night can freeze and blind one. One can't see or feel anything. We can think of this dark energy as masculine or god energy. Again, it can be helpful or hurtful. Zeus, Odin, and Krishna can bring justice, but they can also be ferocious and deadly.

Some people reading this may find it reverses the traditional schema. Most accounts describe the yin, the feminine principle, as dark, and describe the yang, the masculine principle, as light. According to this traditional pattern, then, the Warrior, for example, would be using light, whereas, say, the Love Heals person would be using dark energy. What I've described, which is the opposite of this description, comes from my experience. Perhaps because I tend to go into the dark and to use dark power to meet evil, to attack, I think of yang as the dark energy.

Now, as I've said, we tend toward one type of energy or the other. A Warrior is always going to look for danger and go after it. A Healer is always going to look for hurt and try to love it to wholeness. And when I try to teach for deep change, I want to help people find their way to the elemental energy, to connect with the kind of energy that will help them best use their gifts.

This is not, however, to say that we can't be somewhat fluid. A Warrior's goal is to do good, to protect and serve, and to do that, the Warrior needs to use dark energy. But somehow that dark energy also needs to be brought into the light. That sounds contradictory, but what I mean is that the Warrior will send darkness and danger away by using dark energy, but then can heal the wounds of the person by bringing in the nurturing power of light energy.

Let me give you an example. I had a patient whose father was an alcoholic and abused her. He had died several years before I saw her, but when she came into my office, I could see that he was still attached to her, draining her. I looked at him and had a little talk with him, said, "you're going to be out of here." I let the dark power build and opened the way for him to go. He could see me too. My patient said that she was getting scared, understandably because there was her father's dark presence and all the dark energy I was bringing to the situation. I thought it important for her to do most of the work, so I didn't just get rid of the father. Rather I told him that he was going to leave when she was ready for him to go.

She had to send rage back to him, to heal her own wounds, and to forgive him. These are the three steps necessary for healing. The first, the outer healing, comes from sending back to the being who's harming you whatever emotions you feel toward him or her. Often we hear that we have to forgive the person, but it's hard to forgive someone you're angry at or whom you fear. Simply trying to forgive won't work because there isn't love there. You need to let yourself feel what you feel, tell the other person what you're feeling, and realize the anger or fear is for them, not to be directed at yourself, and if someone is or has been angry at you, you can realize that it's their anger, not yours, and say, "This is your anger, not mine."

Then you can move to the inner healing, healing the wound inside that has been caused by the other person. Often this inner wound is fear, but whatever it is, you are in pain, so you need to comfort, nurture, and love yourself. It's easier to send love to yourself than to someone you fear or hate. If you do both of these steps, you can get to a place of compassion where you truly forgive and separate from the other person.

Think of the connection to the harmful being as like a tree; its roots have taken hold of you and the fear, pain, and anger grow. You need to loosen the soil so that the roots can be taken out. The way to loosen the soil is to direct the hurt, fear, and anger back, then heal/love yourself, and then forgive the one who has caused the hurt. If you don't do all parts of the separation, you are not going to get rid of the other nor of the pain and fear within. Furthermore, without this removal of the roots, you are vulnerable not only to continuing the connection with the other but also to being vulnerable to some other being who wants to attach to you. If you continue to fear abuse, to feel like a victim, you are likely to attract another abuser.

As my patient worked on this process, her father moved farther and farther away because I was standing there and he knew he couldn't get away with anything. Sometimes when I show up, the dark presence just goes, but in this case, as in many others, the roots needed to be released from her energetic field; so she needed to work on getting to the point where she could forgive. If she hadn't, another dark being could have attached to her. At this point, I shifted to my heart chakra and fed her light and love so she would feel safe as she did the work she needed to do. Then I used warmth to heal her aura. In this case, the dark presence of her father did let go and move to the light. If he hadn't, I would have sought other forces in whatever way I was called to do.

In sum, there is the One, the deepest elemental energy. It is expressed in our world, in our experience, as light energy and dark energy. These energies we can focus and use as power. If you want to embrace or to heal, you must express the elemental energy through the power of light. If you want to banish or destroy, you express the elemental energy through the power of dark. Though you may use one at a deeper and more powerful level than the other, though you may connect most naturally with the light or the dark, you can draw on the other depending on what a situation calls for.

What counts in any situation is to connect with the Universal, the elemental energy, and to pause as we sense what we are called to do with it. I'm not sure what this "calling" means. I just know that when I feel around, wait, stay open, I'll get a sense that I'm to move in this or that way, or not to move. How and why this is so, is mysterious. We can't know the One, but we can connect with it and ride its power.

A Path to Healing

A Path to Healing

M y work is all about healing. I didn't always know this, nor did I always understand all healing has to be done from a place of love. It has been a long road. This chapter is my story. As I said in the introduction, it is a road that winds and drifts and has never been direct. There was no master plan; rather I've tried to stay present and let my path direct me. I hope seeing another person's journey helps you find your Way.

I started from a place of pain and darkness. When I was a child, I had dreams and waking visions of dying in a concentration camp. It was only much later I discovered that what I was doing was remembering my immediate previous life. I could see the bricks and smell the gas and hear the screaming. Two powerful seers later told me the camp was Bergen-Belsen between 1938 and 1940. I was told I had been a teenage German Jew, imprisoned with my younger brother. As a child, I was terrified by these visions and didn't understand, and I didn't say anything to anyone about such a fearsome and inexplicable remembrance. When I got a little older, I was drawn to history and read everything I could about the Holocaust. So having been murdered in a concentration camp, I was born into this present life with darkness. Just like Deirdre's my personal karma was dark.

From an early age, I was drawn to very physical contact sports, football, and later lacrosse. One of the seers who saw my previous life in the concentration camp told me my name had been Ari, which means lion. I have always identified myself with hunting animals. I had visions of myself as a wolf, bear, hawk, or lion. And like a hunter, I have always had this energy within me that wanted to attack. Some of the violence was anger from the past and some was my nature's channeling of elemental energy. As I moved on into my teens, though, I felt an impulse to control the violent part of myself. My desire to control this violence was partly instinctual and partly from an unconscious desire not to repeat mistakes from former lives, to avoid repeating my karma, and to shed some of it.

In many past lives, I used my power for ill, to manipulate and gain ascendancy over others. Elsewhere I've described some of the ways I misused Warrior power. After some shamanic training, I also became aware I'd been a sorcerer in previous lives. I've had visions of going back to a room in a tower, a stone library with wooden shelves, a big fireplace, draperies on the wall, and slit windows. As I stayed in the room, one of the walls would shimmer and disappear, and I'd be in another room. In the middle of that room was a lectern with a book on it, not a real book, however. You needed power to open this book and once I'd opened it, instead of pages, it had light and energy which would radiate up from it. It was an experiential book that took me places. It would show me pathways into power. There would be dark horsemen, medieval cavalry, and soldiers. And there were beings from other realms whom I can't describe, who were just power.

Sometimes a dark woman would show up; she was real, someone in one of my past lives. In this past life, we would go together to the tower room. I'd walk in armed with a sword, and she'd walk in wearing a dress made of a dull black material, long and with a tight, laced bodice and long sleeves. She had long black hair and eyes so dark they were almost midnight. We were lovers. We would journey to the tower room, which was a real room in a real tower; then the wall would shimmer and we'd go to the other room with the book. As I said, the book gave me paths to power. It gave her spells, which she would chant for whatever she wanted. For her, the book had pages, which she would turn to whatever spell she wanted. Together we'd use the power to control others for our own purposes.

The room is still there, but I haven't been there for ages.

Even before I knew about these past lives, it was clear to me I needed to control the violence, not let it become destructive to me or to others. Martial arts was the first step.

In my teens, I was attracted to Oriental martial arts not only because they were violent but also because they taught control of the violence. By the time I was twenty, however, I realized that although the martial arts people had great control, their power was too yang, there was too much aggression, and there was no balance. Often masters would drink, do drugs, or have lots of sex as a way to cool that fierce energy.

Then I got into Zen, which not only gave an intense way to focus and control the violence but also indicated a way to gain a spiritual connection. I learned about Zen as a sophomore in college. One of my roommates gave me Phillip Kapleau's *The Three Pillars of Zen*. This was a mind altering book because I had never known anyone would think that way. Kapleau wrote that only direct experience mattered. All else was not really real. I trained very intensely in Japanese Rinzai Zen under Maurine Stuart Roshi. I learned clear focus, discipline, clarity, and ways to channel the aggression mentally and spiritually. Still, there was a lack even here. Many of the Zen masters would be great in the zendo and could move from the bodily to the spiritual brilliantly.

But often they didn't have the mental /emotional level balanced or under control, and therefore when they left the zendo and went out into the everyday world, they would go astray.

What I learned was I needed balance. We have the physical level, the mental/psychological level, and the spiritual level. We need to have balance within each level, and we need balance between the levels. First, consider balance within the levels: On the physical level, you need balance between yin and yang. You need neither to overstimulate nor to starve the physical senses. This kind of balance underlies the medieval idea of balancing the humors or the Buddhist idea of the middle way, being neither ascetic nor overly indulgent.

On the mental/emotional level, you need to balance your emotions, to feel them but not get overly excited, angry, exuberant, nor get overly passive, reactive, depressed. Similarly, you have ideas and can pursue them but should not feed them so much energy that they take over and make you fanatical or monomaniacal.

On the spiritual level, the balance is between light and dark power, using each as appropriate, letting neither carry you so far that it dominates beyond the ability to call on the other. A person too far into light will take off and be ungrounded, a person too far into dark can become ferociously destructive. Either too much light or too much dark can blind you.

Imbalance on any one of these levels can throw off the others. For example, as noted in the Warrior chapter, gurus may be very powerful and balanced on the spiritual level, but when they're not on the meditation cushion, when they're in everyday life, the power has to get expressed in the mind and the body. Instead of using all that power to balance their minds and bodies, they may use it to manipulate. A male guru may have women throwing themselves at him, trying to gain some of his power. If he doesn't focus on the here and now, become aware of what's happening, he may become imbalanced mentally into being flattered and tempted rather than seeing clearly what's happening. Or he may become dominated by lust on the physical level and as we know, this is a very powerful drive that can keep one from being mentally aware of what the reality is. If the guru were balanced so that he could have the mental level clear, he could do something to protect himself and others, for example, setting firm and explicit boundaries, staying committed to a monogamous relationship, etc. Or there's the example of Mother Amah, who is a heart person and has wisely protected herself from being overwhelmed by the needs of those she helps by creating a structure whereby she has assistants running interference for her and by spending only a minute with each person she touches.

This business of not abusing power is one of the main things I focus on in this lifetime.

If you don't balance power on the bodily, mental/emotional, and spiritual levels, you go crazy, sometimes literally, sometimes figuratively. That's why Hebrew mystical training was restricted to those over forty who were married and had children. Similarly, Plato required the rulers in his ideal Republic to undergo long physical, ethical, and intellectual training before they were, at the age of around fifty, allowed to study pure philosophy and apply it as rulers. To deal wisely with such powerful stuff, you need to be mature.

I wasn't there yet, but at this stage I did develop further the means to be aware of power and its uses. For me this was and still is through discipline. I have woken up and meditated every day since I was twenty. I shall always be indebted to Zen for this practice. And I think of it as a practice. I can see doing less some days, more others, or changing the way of meditating. But if you do it, you do it. Buddhists don't ask one another, "Who are you?" so much as "What is your practice?" You need a practice you commit to. For me it's meditating, yoga, Taoist cultivation, and martial arts. For others it may be dance, study, writing, music, healing work with your hands. But whatever it is, in order to make progress, it needs to become a practice.

Where I find people go astray is in their discipline, their practicing, either not doing it consistently or not doing it with awareness and balance. As an example of the latter, the hard part for me is not so much doing the practice as losing the heart by being ultra-focused, ultra disciplined. I find too many people have trouble committing to a practice. They get distracted by the demands of everyday life, they give up when they go through a spell of boredom, or they keep jumping from one practice to another. Whatever your stumbling block may be, I firmly believe you have to have a loving, balanced practice in order to be able to access your power and connect to the Universe.

The next step on my path was realizing that to be balanced, I needed to develop the spiritual more deeply. There's the old observation that when the student is ready, the teacher will appear. As I said, when 1 was twenty, one of my roommates gave me a copy of Kapleau's *Three Pillars of Zen.* What caught me was his explanation that what was important was your own experience of the One, Sartori, or connection to the Universe. This reliance on individual experience took out the middleman. Moreover, here was an enlightened master saying this has been the way far back through generations of teachers, back to the Buddha. Such dharma transmission felt solid and rooted. As a history major in college, this tried and true, established practice felt very good to me.

At the same time, I got attracted to the internal martial arts like t'ai chi and chi gung. Logically this direction made sense, for as one ages, one loses external power but one can keep the internal. But who thinks of this at twenty. Still, since my natural first reaction was to use dark power, at some level I was looking for a way to counter my natural attraction to the dark realms. That's what I'm used to. Years later, a teacher kept telling me, "No violence." I didn't understand that as a young man, but at some level I was looking to change my karma.

After college, I got into healing. Again, the path was circuitous. When I graduated college, I knew I didn't want my career to be teaching martial arts; that was too limited and got boring. Besides I couldn't get people to do what I wanted them to do. How young and arrogant—I had a lot to learn about teaching and helping. After college, the likely tracks were law, business or medicine. Most attracted to medicine, I volunteered at hospitals, became an EMT, worked for a year as an orderly in the operating room; but I didn't like hospitals—too much emotion, too much pain, too much hierarchy. So although I applied to and was accepted by medical schools, in the end, I didn't go.

Once again, I must have been ready because the teacher appeared. My wife was looking through help wanted ads and noticed an ad for an acupuncture teacher requiring many credentials, the kind no American at the time would have had. (The ad was in the newspaper as a requirement for immigration purposes, to prove that there was no local who could do this work and thus prove that the applicant with the skills could immigrate.) I thought, I want to meet this guy. That's how I met Dr. James Tin Yau So. I apprenticed with him, and when he wanted to start an acupuncture school, a group of us started The New England School of Acupuncture.

Obviously my interest in healing, in being a healer and not just a Warrior was growing. I studied and practiced Oriental medicine, which includes acupuncture and herbs, for about ten years. Then I read the second book which had a great influence on my direction: Charles Tart's *Transpersonal Psychology*. I'd studied what was called Far Eastern history, culture, and religion in college. Reading Tart's book was a turning point because it gave me an understanding of how the Eastern traditions I had learned fit into a Western intellectual model. It talked, for example, about ways experiential aspects of Eastern religions related to concepts like ego, id, personality, etc. Learning Western terminology and framework gave me a new way to think about what I'd studied before.

At this point in my career, I actually wasn't interested in shamanism. I had a good acupuncture practice, was teaching, and was most focused on Zen and Taoism for spiritual experience and insight. But I kept dreaming of a lady sitting there beckoning to me; she definitely got my attention because I don't usually have visions in dreams.

A colleague told me that a friend of his had told him about a woman he might be interested in meeting. My colleague insisted that I come to meet this shaman too. My reaction was, "What the hell is that? I don't care about shamanism." Well, I went anyway to keep him happy. We walked in the door, and there she was, the lady who'd been in my dreams. She just looked at me and laughed. My world shifted 180 degrees. I felt as if there had been a shift in the energetic pattern of the universe.

This lady is the one who introduced me to shamanic work, calling souls, separations, aura repair, all the rest. I apprenticed with her for five years. We would see each other, talk with each other, do work together in other realms almost every day. As I worked with patients, I would have ideas and then call her to ask her perceptions and help. She helped me see dark presences and would guide me in ways to release them and to free my patients from them. Together we would journey into other realms so I could learn to see clearly the dark and light sides, the places of power, and the variety of beings who might help with healing work.

As I was learning with her, I read the third book, which influenced me most deeply: *Uncommon Wisdom,* by Frijtof Kapra. This work introduced me to Stanislav Grof, who had done experiments with LSD and had explored the meanings of unconscious experiences of people in altered states. In doing this he came up with a map of the unconscious realms he had studied. As a result of the possibilities he opened, as well as what I was learning with my shaman teacher, I worked to tie together acupuncture, psychology, and shamanism.

I realized if I wanted to work more professionally in this area, I needed more credentials, so I decided to go after a doctorate.

My doctoral dissertation explored the use of acupuncture to induce non-ordinary states of consciousness. I couldn't use shamanism as my scholarly base, since there wasn't enough published on that, so I used Grof's work as a foundation. This study and writing continued simultaneously with my apprenticeship with my shaman teacher.

Another turn in the path came when I was working with a patient who was possessed. I called my teacher and said, "It's evil, and I don't know what to do."

She said, "Call on the patient's soul and we will take a look at the situation together."

So the next morning, around three, when I usually get up, I called the patient's soul, which I could see had darkness around it. I focused on the darkness, and felt my teacher's presence come in.

The power started to vibrate; it built, then there was a big white flash and the dark presence was gone.

Next day I talked with my teacher and said, "That was really cool. What did you do?" She replied, "That wasn't me. That was you."

This experience began my sense of independence and gave me confidence, confidence which was bolstered by my teacher's letting me know that she trusted me. I might make mistakes, but I was sincerely trying to help people, to find ways to heal. As more time went on, I realized she and I had different ways of doing things. Fundamentally, she was of the love heals pattern, and I was a Warrior; so I had to build on what she'd taught me but then go on to develop my own understandings and methods.

The challenge is always how to express the energy I have and use it for good, that is, for healing. And again, healing comes from a place of love. I'm not always that good at sending love; I'd more naturally just attack the enemy. But after attacking the enemy or putting him on notice or whatever other Warrior thing I do, I need to send love to help the person heal. I do so by working inside myself. If someone is in emotional pain, I let myself feel that pain in my own body and heart. Then I try to heal that pain within me, try to heal that pain as I feel it.

Believe it or not, just doing that helps heal the other person. Because I've set up a connection with the other person, having the pain healed in me helps heal it in him. It's like a two-way highway. The way Ho'o ponopono (a Hawaiian form of shamanic healing), puts it, the entire universe is present in everything, so if I heal the pain in me, I heal it in the world. By healing the microcosm, one heals the macrocosm. The Tibetans use a similar technique, called Tonglan meditation. In this system one lets the pain in, transmutes it to love and sends it back out again as compassion, which heals. Another similar method is Metta meditation. Yet another way to think about the connection is that I'm modeling a process for the other person, teaching her to feel the pain, to care for it, and then move to a place of love.

Still, I am attracted to and use dark power. So what I have to work on is being in a place of love, being in my heart. The other comes to me naturally. Conversely, someone who's always in his heart needs to work on dark power, on forceful going out and not just embracing or receiving.

How do I work on getting to that place of love? For me the beginning was meditation, yoga, chi kung, tai chi (the latter two balance my exuberance with the sword and the spear, which I, of course, love). I also try to use inner energy rather than just outward force when I do use the sword and spear. In realms of healing, instead of blasting away, I become patient and wait. Such efforts helped move me toward balance. But more was needed to develop the capacity of love.

As a way of explaining how I've come to develop the capacity to love, let me start with an example from a time about twenty years ago, when I had no clue about all this.

I was working very hard on my internal martial arts, especially their fighting aspect. I was constantly doing drills to increase my ability to do what is called "issuing energy" or Fajing. This involves pushing people and trying not to use muscular strength but rather internal energy. I remember it very clearly. It was winter, so one of my students and I were working in my basement workout room. We had been working for some time and were both warmed up and relaxed. Suddenly, the energy in the room began to buzz and vibrate. I could feel the power building. I touched my student's arm and he just flew across the room and landed against the wall. Neither one of us had any idea what had happened. Over the next few months he and I worked on it until I could do it when I wanted to. The problem was that I could not control it. I would end up hurting him with the power. The power also became addictive. I would want to use it more and more. After a while I became scared of it. It seemed to control me, and it was very tied to my anger and inflicted harm. So I shut it down. The student moved away and I didn't speak of it again for a long time.

As I have thought back on this experience, over time I've come to see that fear, anger, and other negative emotions all can block the ability to use one's power wisely. If you're afraid of your power, as I was, you won't use it or develop it. Or if you're angry and that anger gets mixed up with the use of your power, you'll either misuse the power and hurt someone else and yourself, or you'll fear the anger and not use your power. I also feared that if I used it openly, others might realize I had this power or energy and they'd try to steal it or would judge me harshly.

Finally I realized that the power was there and that I had to do something with it. So as not to hurt someone else, and so as to protect myself, I went to other realms with it, realms where I could try to use it for healing. For example, I would use aggressive energy to help get rid of possession.

Probing more deeply, I found that anger and fear often come from a negative internal dialogue. Everyone I've met has this kind of conversation with him- or herself. You know what I mean. Even in a trivial matter like dropping and breaking a glass, your first reaction may be something like "you idiot" or "that was stupid" or in the very voice of a parent, "you wouldn't do things like that if you'd just pay attention." We all carry baggage from the past that encourages us to be hard on ourselves.

If we can ease this internal dialogue, we can ease the negative emotions that block us from using our power. How do we do this? By loving ourselves. I've found that when you work on loving yourself, the ferocity of the internal dialogue lessens. And when these negative emotions ease, the fear and anger that block us from our power dissipate.

Ok, all the self-help books say "love yourself," "do affirmations," and "be as gentle with yourself as you would be with someone else." This can seem like narcissism or downright denial of reality. After all, sometimes we really are stupid or mean or inept or even evil; and it's a rare person who doesn't sometimes have hateful thoughts.

Let's go back to the small example of the glass you've just dropped and broken. Say your spontaneous reaction is to be angry at yourself. You could start by noticing that you're angry at yourself, and catch the negative internal dialogue. Then you might say, "Well, the glass isn't really that important." This may be true, but it's still not being compassionate with yourself for breaking the glass and for being angry at yourself and calling yourself names. Then you could send love to the part of yourself that's angry. What words you use aren't important. Sometimes I say "I love you," or I might send love to the glass that I broke. Other times, I say, "Let all beings be in love." Or you could say a prayer, recite a line from a poem or from the Bible, or sing to yourself. One experienced meditator says to herself something like "Sweetheart, you're upset, now let it go, you broke a glass and you're going to deal with that." It doesn't matter, so long as you speak with kindness. After a while, the next time you drop a glass, you'll just feel that you've dropped a glass.

A Buddhist way to think about this is to see that thoughts and feelings aren't real. They're real thoughts and feelings, certainly, but they are only thoughts and feelings. The fact is I dropped the glass. The feeling is my addition to the fact. If I think I'm a jerk, and feel like a jerk, and dwell on those responses, the thoughts and feelings become stronger. If you feed these thoughts and feelings, they become stronger. But if you replace them with love, they become love. If you're feeling love, it's difficult to feel anger or fear. We can feel more than one emotion at a time, but we can also shift the focus of which ones we give energy to.

I'm not quite sure how it works, there's a leap here, but experientially, I've found that as you work on loving yourself, and as the negative emotions lose strength, the fear of your power dissipates.

Now you may think here that loving one's self is just another emotion, maybe a more pleasant one than fear or anger, but still a way that we hold on to the ego. You may remember from earlier chapters that to connect with the Universe means to let ourselves, to let our egos go; and our egos are used to being in charge, used to determine how we function in the world. We do need a strong ego to function in the everyday world. So how does loving ourselves help us connect with the Universe? Why doesn't it just make the ego stronger? I'm not sure, but what I think may be the case is that, first, true compassion toward self as well as toward others doesn't block us, doesn't close us off the way negative emotions do.

Second, although love on one level can be narcissistic, grasping, desirous, and attaching, it can also be something greater than a self-based emotion. It can transcend the self. There are two kinds of love: the emotion of love and the love that comes through us from a higher level. As you may recall, the power of the Universe in itself is neutral, but as it manifests in the world, it becomes the two, in Taoist terms—light and dark, aggression and embracing, cold and hot, yin and yang. We can choose which kind of power we want to let come through us (remembering that we have differing gifts that refract the power in different ways). And we may manifest different powers at different times; I switch back and forth as seems to be needed. Thus we can connect to a higher power of love. We can let a higher power of love (call it god, holy spirit, divine mother, Kuan Yin, whatever) come through us.

There's another way that the ego can become more elastic and more accepting, less worried and tight. Simply getting older. There's an Asian belief that life has three stages: in the first, one is learning; in the second, one is working, raising a family, making one's way in the world; in the third, one can move away from these demands and reflect, perhaps become wise.

In Western terms, when you're young, your ego is invested in being the best, in controlling everything, and in not losing your abilities or position or security. As you get older, you can become more accepting, less rigid, and more open to other possibilities. Older people may not get so agitated about things that used to seem of huge importance. When we're older, we've made many life decisions, many paths not taken are behind us, and we don't have to worry about them anymore. Furthermore, when you've done something for a long time, you may get mellower about it, and more accepting of other people's ways of doing it. My teacher works one way, I work another, that's cool. I'm not trying to minimize the pains of aging, nor am I saying that all people can age gracefully. But as we get older, in spite of all the physical world concerns about failing senses, illness, and such, at another level, there can be less fear.

You have a choice. You can live in love or you can live in fear.

Afterword

I was awakened last night by the full moon shining through my window. I got up and went outside. The day before had been 60 degrees and pouring rain. Washed all the snow away. A front must have come through because it was back in the 20s. Cold and clear. A perfect time to see. Cold, clear moonlight. On this kind of night, I am able to go to the place where I see, which is also cold and clear, and connect to the Universe with ease.

A friend tells me that even under the frozen earth she can feel the stirrings of spring. Tiny roots are starting to uncurl deep under the surface. She thinks ahead to when she'll lie on a warm beach, the sun sensual on her body, and go easily to the place where she feels the energy of the Universe move through her.

Whether you're a seer or a feeler, I hope this book's descriptions of the ways people connect and of the patterns that flow from the connection have been helpful.

May you find peace, love, and happiness in your journey.

February Full Moon, 2008

Suggested Readings

Bates, Brian. *The Real Middle Earth*. New York: Palgrave MacMillan, 2002.

_____. *The Way of Wyrd*. New York: Harpercollins, 1992.

Bhagavadgita. Trans. Stephen Mitchell. New York: Three Rivers Press, 2000.

Blofeld, John. *Taoism: The Road to Immortality*. Boston: Shambhala, 1978.

Bolen, Jean Shinoda. *Goddesses in Everywoman*. New York: Harper and Row, 1984.

_____. *Gods in Everyman*. New York: Harper and Row, 1989.

Campbell, Joseph. *The Power of Myth*. New York: Doubleday, 1988.

Canizares, Raul. *Walking with the Night: The Afro-Cuban World of Santeria*. Rochester, VT: Destiny Books, 1993.

Capra, Fritjof. *The Tao of Physics*. Boston: Shambhala, 1975.

_____. *Uncommon Wisdom*. New York: Bantam. 1989.

Castaneda, Carlos. *Journey to Ixtalan*. New York: Simon and Schuster, 1972.

_____. *Tales of Power*. New York: Simon and Schuster, 1974.

Chuang Tsu. *Inner Chapters*. Trans. Gia-Fu Feng and Jane English. New York: Vintage, 1974.

Dalai Lama. *The Universe in a Single Atom: The Convergence of Science and Spirituality*. New York: Morgan Road Books, 2005.

Danos, Kosta. *The Magus of Java*. Rochester, VT: Inner Traditions, 2000.

Dunn, James. *Wisdom of the Soul: The Kabbalah of Rabbi Isaac Luria*. Newburyport, MA: Weiser Books, 2008.

Estes, Clarissa Pinkola. *Women Who Run with the Wolves*. New York: Ballantine Books, 1992.

Fulford, Robert. *Dr. Fulford's Touch of Life*. New York: Pocket Books, 1996.

Hanh, Thich Nhat. *Old Path White Clouds: Walking in the Footsteps of the Buddha*. Berkeley, CA: Parallax Press, 1991.

Harner, Michael. *The Way of the Shaman*. San Francisco and New York: Harper and Row, 1980.

Herrigel, Eugen. *Zen and the Art of Archery*. New York: Vintage Press, 1999.

Hesse, Hermann. *Siddhartha*. New York: New Directions, 1951.

Hildegard of Bingen. *Book of Divine Works*. Ed. Matthew Fox. Santa Fe: Bear and Co., 1987.

Hoff, Benjamin. *The Tao of Pooh*. New York: Penguin, 1982.

Kapleau, Philip. *The Three Pillars of Zen*. Boston: Beacon Press, 1965.

Keeney, Bradford. *Bushman Shaman*: Awakening the Spirit through Ecstatic Dance. Rochester VT: Destiny Books, 2005.

Kottler, Jeffrey, and Jon Carlson. *American Shaman*. New York: Brunner-Routledge, 2004.

Krishnamurti. *On Fear*. New York: HarperOne, 1995.

Lame Deer, Archie Fire. *Gift of Power*. Santa Fe: Bear and Co., 1994.

Lao Tsu. *Tao Te Ching*. Trans. Gia-Fu Feng and Jane English. New York: Vintage Books, 1972.

Lawlor, Robert. *Voices of the First Day: Awakening in the Aboriginal Dreamtime*. Rochester, VT: Inner Traditions, 1991.

Markides, Kyriacos C. *The Magus of Sgtrovolos*. New York: Penguin, 1985.

Matthews, Caitlin and John. *Walkers between the Worlds: The Western Mysteries from Shaman to Magus*. Rochester, VT: Inner Traditions, 2003.

Mountain, Marian. *The Zen Environment: The Impact of Zen Meditation*. Bantam Books: New York, 1983.

Musashi, Miyamoto. *A Book of Five Rings*. Woodstock, NY: Overlook Press, 1982.

Myerson, John, and Robert Greenebaum. *Riding the Spirit Wind*. Framingham, MA: Life Arts Press, 2003.

Nan, H. C. *Tao and Longevity: Mind-Body Transformation*. Newburyport, MA: Weiser, 1984.

Neihardt, John G. *Black Elk Speaks; Being the Life Story of a Holy Man of the Oglala Sioux*. Lincoln, NE: University of Nebraska Press, 1961.

Profiles in Healing Series. Ed. Bradford Keeney. Philadelphia: Ringing Rocks Press.

Balians: Traditional Healers of Bali
Gary Holy Bull: Lakota Yuwipi Man
Guarani Shamans of the Forest
Hands of Faith: Healers of Brazil
Ikuko Osumi, Sensei: Japanese Master of Seiki Jutsu
Kalahari Bushmen Healers
Ropes to God: Experiencing the Bushman Spiritual Universe
Shakers of St. Vincent
Vusamazulu Credo Mutwa: Sulu High Sanusi
Walking Thunder: Dine Medicine Women

Ritchie, Mark Andrew. *Spirit of the Rain Forest: A Yanomamo Shaman's Story*. Chicago: Island Lake Press, 2000.

Salzberg, Sharon. *Lovingkindness: The Revolutionary Art of Happiness*. Boston: Shambhala, 2008.

Some, Malidoma. *Of Water and the Spirit*. New York: Tardier, 1994.

Soygul Rinpoche. *The Tibetan Book of Living and Dying*. San Francisco: Harper, 1984.

Starhawk. *The Spiral Dance*. Boston: Beacon, 1978.

Steinsaltz, Adin. *The Thirteen Petalled Rose: A Discourse on the Essence of Jewish Existence and Belief*. New York: Basic Books, 2006.

Stevens, John. *Abundant Peace:* The *Biography of Morihei Ueshiba, Founder of Akido*. Boston: Shambhala, 1987.

_____. *The Sword of No* Sword: *Life of the Master Warrior Tesshu*. Boston: Shambhala, 1989.

Stozzi-Heckler, Richard. *In Search of the* Warrior *Spirit: Teaching Awareness Discipline to the Green Berets*. Berkeley: North Atlantic Books, 2003.

Suzuki, Shunryu. *Zen Mind,* Beginner's *Mind*. New York and Tokyo: Weatherhill, 1970.

Tart, Charles. Transpersonal *Psychologies: Perspectives on the Mind from Seven Great Spiritual Traditions*. New York: HarperCollins, 1992.

The Zen Teaching of Huang *Po*. Trans. John Blofeld. New York: Grove Press, 1958.

Trungpa, Chogyam. Shambhala: *The Sacred Path of the Warrior*. Boston: Shambhala, 1984.

Van der Wettering, Janwillem. *After Zen*. New York: St. Martin's Press, 1999.

_____. *The Empty Mirror*. Boston: Houghton Mifflin, 1973.

_____. *A Glimpse of Nothingness*. Boston: Houghton Mifflin, 1975.

Welch, Holmes. Taoism: *The Parting of the Way*. Boston: Beacon, 1965.

Whitaker, Kay. *The Reluctant Shaman*. New York: Harper Collins, 1991.

Wolf, Fred Alan. *The Eagle's Quest: A Physicist Finds the Scientific Truth at the Heart of the Shamanic World*. New York: Touchstone, 1991.

About the Authors

John G. Myerson, Ph.D., Lie. Ac., is a graduate of Harvard College and the New England School of Acupuncture. He received his Doctorate in Psychology from The Union Institute. He practices shamanic healing, psychotherapy, and Oriental medicine and is the founder of the LifeArts Center for Healing and Shamanic Studies in Framingham, Massachusetts. He has studied, practiced, and taught Zen, yoga, Taoist cultivation, martial arts, and shamanic practices for over forty years.

Judith Robbins studied Philosophy and Literature at Harvard University (A.B., M.A.T.). As well as teaching in these areas for over forty years, she has also studied, practiced, and taught Vipassana meditation, tai chi, yoga, and shamanic healing. Most recently, she co-authored the sixth edition of *Writing a Research Paper,* published in 2008 by Wayside Press.

www.ingramcontent.com/pod-product-compliance
Lightning Source LLC
Chambersburg PA
CBHW072143020426
42334CB00018B/1861